Central American Writers of West Indian Origin

A New Hispanic Literature

Central American Writers of West Indian Origin
A New Hispanic Literature

Ian Smart

Three Continents

Three Continents Press
1346 Connecticut Avenue, N.W.
Washington, D.C. 20036

ISBN: 0-89410-397-0
ISBN: 0-89410-398-9 (pbk)
LC No: 83-50205

Cover photograph shows deck of the
Ancón at Cristóbal, Canal Zone,
September, 1909, crowded with a newly
arrived "cargo" of 1500 West Indians.

*To my parents and my eleven brothers
and sisters in the flesh;
To Buena Isidra and her people, my long-lost
cultural brothers and sisters;
And to Monifa Isidra, the bringer of luck,
the "antiscatterer."*

There are many scholars whose direct or indirect influence has contributed significantly to my intellectual formation, and, consequently, to this book. I am singularly grateful to them all. I shall dare to list some of them, a mere representative sample, in more or less chronological order of their impact on me:

José Luis Gonzáles, María del Carmen Millán, the late Professor Donald F. Fogelquist, Mervyn C. Alleyne, Mazizi Kunene, Kenneth Ramchand, Wilfred G. Cartey, Richard L. Jackson, Edward Kamau Brathwaite, Martha K. Cobb, George Lamming, Isabelo Zenón Cruz, Lemuel A. Johnson, Adalberto Ortiz, Stanley A. Cyrus, Donald E. Herdeck, Roy S. Bryce LaPorte, Isidore Okpewho, Maurice A. Lubin, Angel Augier, Nancy Morejón, and, above all, Henry J. Richards.

I owe a particular debt to Henry for his masterful assistance in the preparation of this manuscript.

Amo a mi raza
porque tú quieres que la olvide
que la reniegue
que la ignore
que acepte que ni siquiera
debe pertenecerme.

Gerardo Maloney, from "Amo a mi raza" (1983)

CONTENTS

ILLUSTRATIONS

AUTHOR'S FOREWORD

Them is one race
  The Caribbean man
From the same place
  The Caribbean man
That make the same trip
  The Caribbean man
On the same ship
  The Caribbean man.

*From "Caribbean Man, a 1979
calypso by Black Stalin*

This incursion into the still practically unexplored domains of West Indian literary criticism will focus substantially on literary expressions emanating from Panama and Costa Rica, lands that I have come to know and love dearly. The work, then, might more accurately, but far less elegantly, have been titled, "A Study of Some West Indian Writers from Two Central American Countries—Panama and Costa Rica—with Some Reference to West Indian Literature from Other Central American Countries."

The limits of this study, essentially a ground-breaking enterprise, enhance its validity, for the line of approach used and the resulting insights derived can serve as models for further critical explorations of the burgeoning field of West Indian literature from Central America. What is true for the literature from Panama and Costa Rica to be reviewed in this work should be true for analogously produced literature from Nicaragua (some of which we shall discuss briefly in the Conclusion), Guatemala, Honduras, Colombia, Venezuela, Cuba, the Dominican Republic, or any land in the general Caribbean region where a peculiar demographic cross-pollination has resulted in the creation of Hispanic literature by Caribbean peoples whose culture and history are profoundly rooted in the English-speaking islands.

This leads to yet another clarification and limitation. My study is concerned only with Hispanic literature, that is, literature of Spanish expression. It thereby excludes from its purview the entire and most interesting phenomenon of Belizian literature.

Finally, I have used the term "West Indian" with the intention of being calculatingly provocative, hoping to generate light as well as heat. To this end, I have been careful to attempt a precise definition of the term at the end of my Introduction.

The development of the work will follow a fundamental principle of intellectual inquiry, that of proceeding from the general to the particular. Thus, the introduction will provide the essential sociohistorical background, and the first chapter will extend the examination of that background to include those non-West Indian writers who first began to treat "West Indian" life and culture in a literary fashion, writing "West Indians" into the fabric of their fiction. The second and third chapters will study two crucial areas in which "West Indianness" flourishes in the literature under consideration, namely, language and religion. The chapter on religion will center on the works of Quince Duncan. The remaining chapters of the body of the work will focus on those contemporary Central American "West Indian" writers whose works show the greatest promise: Cubena (Carlos Guillermo Wislon) in Chapter Four along with Gerardo Maloney, Eulalia Bernard, and the other blossoming poets in Chapter Five. The final chapter will present as its essential thrust a look towards the future and an exploration of the possibility of a truly pan-Caribbean literature. (The reader is advised that at the end of Chapter One he will find a restatement of this overall plan in the more specific language that is more appropriately employed *in medias res.*)

The approach throughout the book will conform fully to the generally accepted canons of literary scholarship. It is my firm contention that the body of works studied in this book is first and foremost a body of belles lettres, and, as such, makes its primary contribution in the area of aesthetics. A full appreciation of this contribution then can only be gained through insight into the form and content of the works as art. However, a wide diversity of factors, as wide as the range of human experience, impinges upon the form and content of any artistic product. No literary study can a priori exclude any of these factors, and all such factors included must be of clearly demonstrable relevance to the greater artistic appreciation of the work under consideration.

My study is a modest beginning, but I hope that its impact will be much more far-reaching than I should dare to expect. West Indian literary criticism is still, alas, in a fledgling state that gives rise in some quarters to disturbing suspicions of retardation, perhaps congenital. A work such as this one fills then a material need by adding to the number of printed pages dedicated exclusively to the criticism of West Indian literature. Hopefully, it will, in addition, bring to English-speaking West Indians not only word of the existence of their Spanish-speaking counterparts, but, as well, a profound appreciation of the literature of these Hispanophones who are doubly brothers and fully Caribbean. It is my hope that my book will thereby contribute to the cause of Caribbean unity, the true sense that indeed "all of we is one." I further dare to hope that the excitement thus generated will stimulate further literary investigation that will fill out the fledgling corpus of West Indian literary criticism, and dispell forever the doubts about its developmental normalcy.

This book is, then, part of a process that is itself a constituent element of a much larger whole, to wit, the humanistic enterprise.

INTRODUCTION: THE "SCATTERATION" TO CENTRAL AMERICA

Where then is the nigger's
home?

In Paris Brixton Kingston
Rome?

Edward Kamau Brathwaite

A mere look at a map of the Caribbean will leave the viewer with the strong impression of the geographical unity of the region, a string of islands and rimlands of Central and South America that encircle the Caribbean Sea. A survey of the history of the region will further confirm this impression of unity. C. L. R. James, the noted historian and political commentator, has succintly summed up the history of the islands in the terms, "sugar and slavery." Whereas the commonness of the geographical and historical experiences of the islands is readily accepted by most people, the inclusion of the Central and South American rimlands into the Caribbean consciousness is not quite so common. The fact is, however, that the socioeconomic reality summed up in "sugar and slavery" conditioned the historical process of much of the rimland regions as well. Thus the plantation model dominates in Caribbean rimland areas of Colombia, Venezuela, Mexico, and certainly, as of the later neocolonial stage (i.e. subsequent to independence from Spain), in Panama, Costa Rica, Guatemala (Belize), Nicaragua, and Honduras. The fact is, too, that just as there have been constant lines of communication among the peoples of all the islands over the five centuries of their colonial and neocolonial existence, there have been similar continuing contacts among the islands and the rimlands over the course of the same period.[1] This book will dwell on the significance of the phenomenon for Panama and Costa Rica, but will also indicate that the situation in Panama and Costa Rica is certainly duplicated in Nicaragua, Honduras, Guatemala, and of course has produced its most unique political results in Belize.

History records the dispersal of several waves of population from the islands to the rimlands. The very conquest of Mexico, the exploration and colonization of Panama, can be considered the earliest manifestations. The case of the Black Caribs, expelled from St. Vincent at the end of the eighteenth century and banished to what is now Belize, is yet another example.[2] The California Gold Rush triggered the first significant demographic interaction between Panama and the islands of the Anglophone Caribbean. The discovery of California gold motivated the construction of the transisthmian railroad (1850-55), the labor force for which came primarily from the ranks of the newly emancipated Caribbean slaves—mostly from Jamaica—weary of the traditional forms of the plantation and ripe for inducement into the web of the more evolved forms. This successful experiment with immigrant West Indian labor was repeated in 1872, when Costa Rica chose to seek the advantages of rail transportation between the tropical Caribbean coast and the coffee plantations and settlements of the central plateau region.[3]

In the 1880's Panama was again the focus of a wave of immigration from the Caribbean islands when the French attempted unsuccessfully to build a sea-level canal. The United Fruit Company—itself a by-product of West Indian immigration to Costa Rica[4]—established banana plantations in the Bocas del Toro region on Panama's Caribbean coast bordering on Costa Rica, in 1889. This development attracted immigrant workers, mostly Jamaicans. Finally, consequent on their engineering of Panama's independence, the ruling forces of the United States successfully arranged the building of the Panama Canal, between 1904 and 1914. During these ten years, many thousands of new immigrant workers flowed into Panama from Barbados, Jamaica, Trinidad and Tobago, as well as Haiti, St. Lucia, Martinique, Guadeloupe and other islands. This wave of immigration proved to be the most intense, giving final shape to the socioeconomic characteristics of the Panamanian nation. The 1939-45 war and the necessary works on the defenses of the Canal attracted a new wave of immigrants and ushered in a period of prosperity in Panama, the second and perhaps the last one to be generated by the Canal.

Neither in colonial Panama nor Costa Rica (and this is generally true for the rest of Central America) was there any significant development of the plantation system of slavery. However, in Panama, the descendants of Africans constitute the overwhelming majority of the population,[5] and consequently have had a considerable cultural impact on this nation. Their impact is far less significant, but equally real, in Costa Rica.[6] Those black Panamanians whose roots date back to the colonial period are referred to as *negros coloniales*, (colonial blacks) to distinguish them from the newer Caribbean immigrants: the *negros antillanos* (the Antillean blacks), *antillanos*, *afro-antillanos*, *afro-antillanos panameños* (Afro-Antillean Panamanians), *criollos*, or *chombos*,[7] as they have been called—along with many other things. Costa Rica does not generally recognize her own version of *negros coloniales*, so that, in effect, the new immigrants constitute a separate group as well, being the only generally recognized *negros* in contemporary Costa Rica. The separation of the "new" West Indian immigrants and their descendants from the "old" African demographic elements in Panama and Costa Rica is, then, one of the most important ingredients in the fashioning of the present-day situation.

It can be asserted that the West Indian immigrants and their descendants in Panama and Costa Rica constitute an ethnolinguistic minority group. Of the many theories generated by the numerous social scientists who have studied the problems of such groups, that of the North American researcher Manuel Ramirez, III appears to be the most helpful. His approach posits two basic models for the resolution of the basic problems of ethnolinguistic minority groups: the Conflict-Replacement and the Flexibility-Synthesis models.[8] Our book focuses primarily on literature produced by members of the third generation (approximately speaking) of the ethnolinguistic minority group in Panama and Costa Rica. It appears from the research published so far on the matter of their religion, education, economic and political status that this ethnolinguistic minority group is faced almost exclusively with the Conflict-Replacement dilemma.[9] In other words, the host societies reaction to them is one that is basically conflict inducing and conducive to the abdication of their cultural autonomy.

The preceding analysis of the condition of those immigrants (and their descendants) who went from the islands of the Caribbean to Central America leads ultimately to the complex question of the appropriate designation or designations for this group of human beings.

The Question of Names

The term "West Indian" applies in the fullest possible sense to the literature to be studied, since it is produced by a group of people who have maintained strong cultural ties with the islands of their immediate provenience, namely, the Caribbean islands. The majority of these people came from Jamaica, Barbados, Trinidad and Tobago, Grenada, St. Kitts, St. Vincent, etc. and were thus English-speaking. Some, however, were French Creole speakers coming from Haiti, Martinique, Guadeloupe, and such islands as Dominica and St. Lucia (officially supposed to be English-speaking). The fact is that throughout the history of their stay in both Panama and Costa Rica they have been perceived as all coming generally from Jamaica, and have indeed constantly been referred to as simply: *"jamaicanos," "jamaiquinos,"* or more derisively, *"chumecaman,"* or *"chumeca"* (see note 7)—terms representing the English Creole pronunciation of "Jamaica." Certainly, then, in the narrowest sense of the term, such people are "West Indian."

There is a custom among English speakers to reserve the term "West Indian" for the largely Anglophone African population of certain islands. Serious questions arise about the legitimacy of this practice. It appears to be based on a distinction that is posited solely on the basis of the language of the colonial master and must then be considered ill-advised, for it would ignore the common African cultural base as well as the common historical experience. The trend of modern scholars has been to do away with the divisiveness imposed by the Euro-based fragmentation of the Caribbean. We cite in support of this view the ground-breaking studies: *Race and Colour in Caribbean Literature* (1960), and *Black Images* (1970), by G. R. Coulthard and Wilfred G. Cartey respectively. More recently Franklin W. Knight (*The Caribbean, 1978*) and Selwyn Cudjoe (*Resistance and Caribbean Literature,* 1980) have contributed to the strengthening of this trend. There is then no reason why "West Indian" should not be entirely synonymous with "*antillais*" or "*antillano*", the respective French and Spanish versions.

The term "West Indian," furthermore, has a real but frequently unstated connotation of Blackness. In this sense it is used in contrast to "Caribbean" with the unstated assumption that "Caribbean" does not necessarily imply exclusive Africanity since it may also suggest "Latin" rather than "African." This reasoning is simply unscientific, unsupported by the facts, for the majority of the people in the Caribbean area are, in fact, of African origin. The African cultural heritage constitutes one of the defining features of Caribbeanness even in the fullest geographical sense, for the African cultural note is the dominant one, or one of the most prominent, in the peculiar culture of all of the islands and rimland regions considered to be Caribbean.

The term "West Indian" can then be entirely synonymous with "Caribbean."[10] This affirmation may run counter to the sensibilities of many people, but it is solidly logical. Strictly speaking, then, the "West Indian" literature that will be examined in this book, while it has a very special relation to Anglophone Caribbean literature, also, like the latter, pertains to a larger and coherently ordered body of literature that can be termed "Caribbean," "Pan-Caribbean," or even, according to the reasoning outlined above, just simply, "West Indian."

The considerations presented in these last few paragraphs are perhaps the most important contribution this book can make. They will be restated in a more evolved form in the concluding chapter.

CHAPTER ONE

THE NON-WEST INDIAN PRECURSORS

There is a group of Central American writers who, while being neither biologically nor culturally "West Indian," have been creatively influenced by the West Indian presence. This chapter will explore the different levels of that influence on the form and content of the art of those writers, most especially in the area of characterization. It will also examine how the influence is reflected in the output of the new West Indian author.

The Works

Joaquín Beleño C.: the View From Beneath the Bed

Joaquín Beleño C. (b. 1922), from Panama, is the most important of this group of non-West Indian Central American authors. Precisely because the West Indian presence is so strongly felt in his novels, they have met with some degree of opposition from his countrymen. Rodrigo Miró, for example, the establishment literary figure par excellence, quite bluntly affirms: "Beleño through the words and actions of some of his characters at times purports to represent 'Panamanianness.' His attempts fall short of being authentic, for the heroes he presents us are of questionable 'Panamanianness'."[1] The critic Mélida Ruth Sepúlveda presents the diametrically opposed point of view. She see Beleño as creating one of the most important fictional characters in Panamanian literature—Atá (Arthur), of *Gamboa Road Gang*. With the creation of Atá, "for the first time a Panamanian author successfully portrays a man struggling with himself and with his environment to belong to a human and social group which rejects him."[2] This view is shared by another critic, Jorge Turner (the name would suggest that he is himself of Anglophone Caribbean ancestry), who wrote the prologue to the edition of the novel published upon its winning the first prize at the 1959 Ricardo Miró Contest. Turner asserts that he is himself echoing the view of a certain Dr. Ferrer Valdés when he states that the character Atá "is the most real and complete creation to come out of the literature from the isthmus."[3] *Gamboa Road Gang* is the last of Beleño's trilogy of novels on the Canal theme. The other two are, *Curundú*, which was written between 1943 and 1946 but not published until 1963 and which won one of the prizes in the 1956 Miró Contest, and *Luna Verde*, published in 1951.

The road that leads to Atá is a long and well-defined one. Tracing it will contribute to our understanding of not only Beleño's art but of the creativity of all the other non-West Indian writers who, even before any *antillano* could do so, included on their artistic agenda the portrayal of West Indian life as it presented itself in Central America.

One of the most important aspects, in fact, the fundamental one for a novelist, in the portrayal of West Indian life is the characterization of West Indian figures. Accurate portrayal of that life will make for successful characterization, and this latter will be the hallmark of the former. The capacity for observation is basic, so that the process of observation is also overwhelmingly significant. *Curundú*, the first novel written by Beleño, provides the reader with a scene which gives poignant insight into the process of observation. It can be considered a self-portrait of the artist as observer, and as such is a vital key to the understanding of this aspect of his creativity.

The scene is placed at the beginning of the second third of the novel (pp. 119 to 132), one narrated on the basis of flashbacks and the fevered reminiscences of the main character, Rubén Galván. It occupies a whole chapter, the tenth of twenty-three, entitled, "Oh Cristí! Oh Cristí! Aleluya!" In it Rubén reminisces on the occasion when, as a young boy, he entered stealthily into the adjoining room of one of his West Indian neighbors, Cristí, shortly after the latter's death, to observe what was taking place from his favorite vantage point, a hiding place beneath a bed—an old-fashioned one with springs.

This scene of the view from beneath the bed is highly symbolic, containing all the elements of Beleño's treatment of West Indians, and presenting the exact psychological dimensions of their impact on the *latino* community.[4] It does so mainly because of the author's immensely successful device of having a child look in on the intimacies of the others' world from the privileged position beneath the bed, where he is protected from all adult interference. The hiding place is itself extremely intimate and comforting. It furthermore creates in Rubén a particularly sensitized state of consciousness that makes him especially receptive to all external stimuli, thus generating immense empathy with what he observes. It is his intimate excitement, his "sweet feeling of fear mixed with pleasure,"[5] that both symbolizes and manifests this special receptiveness, and so the author refers to it again and again throughout the scene. Rubén the child observer is an outsider who has come as close to the inside as is possible. He is an observer entirely without prejudice, open only to the impact of the stimuli that impinge upon all his senses.

Because of the novel's style this optimum observer attitude of the child can be juxtaposed impressively to the prejudiced, nonobserver attitude of the adult, significantly in this case, of Rubén's mother. Beneath the bed Rubén recalls his earlier contacts with Cristí, "the 'Jamaican' who used to give him a five-cent piece or buy him some bun, a sort of West-Indian sweet bread." His spontaneous reaction to these acts of kindness is contrasted with his mother's attitude, one of mechanical rejection bred of blind, unreasoned prejudice: "His mother would get angry because, according to her, the *chombos* made their sweet bread with 'water used to wash the dead'" (p. 122). the mother's attitude will cast its shadow on the child's, stamping him with an ambivalence that will persist throughout.

This ambivalence, indeed, taints all of Rubén's dealings with the West Indian characters with whom he is made to interact in the novel, and it could reasonably be argued that his experiences and attitudes closely reflect those of the author. The plot of the novel can be summarized simply. Rubén Galván, a student at the highest level of preuniversity education, goes to work on the Canal Zone during the long holidays. He is caught up in the contagious excitement generated by the money and general moral relaxation fostered by the Yankee presence in Panama. This circumstance provides Beleño with the basis for his impassioned defense of Panamanian sovereignty faced with the Yankee menace. Thus Rubén's experiences on the job constitute the essence of the plot. The author skillfully makes them mesh with a poignant factor in Rubén's family history, the displacement of his family, his grandmother and uncle, from their land. The connection is then both eminently symbolic and materially well-executed. It turns out that at the work place Fulo Alejandro, a dissolute, white-skinned bourgeois Panamanian, the son of a corrupt politician, is the middleman between the Yankee bosses and the native workers. It is his family that has purchased the land that Rubén's grandmother, now deceased, and uncle consider to be an inviolable family birthright. Fulo is forced to be the eventual evictor when his sister drives him to action, since she needs the rent from the land to assure the future of her child—symbolically fathered by her white North American husband. Rubén discovers almost by accident the details of this infernal machination of destiny and is killed along with his uncle in the attempt to salvage the last vestige of the family's material honor. Rubén's experiences as he works on the Canal Zone can themselves be reduced essentially to his interaction with the various characters he encounters, many of whom are West Indians.

For the purposes of our analysis the three most relevant West Indian characters are Liequí, Tamtam, and Red Box, who appears briefly but is of immense significance since he points the way most directly to Atá. The instinctive attraction that Rubén feels towards these West Indians is clearly documented. On the job the men sorted themselves into groups "as if by instinct, but Rubén sought the company of Tamtam and Liequí because he found their companionship pleasing" (p. 167). The reason for this attraction bears watching, however, for the author explains that "he [Rubén] finds a certain *perverse* warmth in their actions" (p. 167, emphasis added). Thus the author goes on to say that the young impressionable adolescent, Rubén, "tries to learn Tamtam's aggressive ways, with that discreet hostility of the bad guys of the screen, to the point of imitating him without realizing it" (p. 167). The boy from beneath the bed instinctively admires the manly style of his young West Indian companion. However, the mother's attitude imposes itself and these very positive qualities are seen as tainted with a certain perversity. Similarly, Beleño the author is obviously attracted to the West Indian life style, finding it warm, human, exciting, but the attraction is something to be guarded against because these West Indians, his prejudice dictates, are essentially inferior and imperfect.

It is with the creation of Red Box that Beleño first attains the high point in characterization along the road forged by the view from beneath the bed. He enters the novel dramatically as an eminently sympathetic defender of the downtrodden workers. His role in this respect is quite clear. The author states: "But the personality of the crazy Red Box strongly attracted him [Rubén] ... because he was an ally against his two compatriots who used to humiliate him" (p. 174). Red Box sweeps the young Rubén into a new kind of confrontation with the Yankee oppressor, giving his life an added dimension of excitement and insight. But this crazy, colorful character is one of the most tragic of West Indian characters, a traumatized mulatto, a perfect *chombo blanco* (white *chombo*). The illegitimate son of one of the North American oppressors and a West Indian woman, he has theoretical U.S. citizenship that he can never convert into any significant material advantage, and he certainly does not consider himself Panamanian. Furthermore, he despises the very group that he must belong to, not only by the process of elimination, but because this group warmly wishes to embrace him, namely, the *chombos*. The only possible consequence of Red Box's untenable situation is madness, and he is in fact quite mad.

The West Indian characters of *Curundú* are then basically sympathetic. However, the work is laced with statements of prejudiced antipathy towards West Indians in general. They are seen as turncoats, collaborating with the oppressor because they have no loyalty to Panama, and because they are substantially spineless sycophants. These opinions are aired in the scenes of petty bickering almost at the level of teenage banter between Rubén and Salvador Brown, his erstwhile fellow student now his co-worker and an obtrusively prosletyzing born-again Christian fresh from a period of seminary training in the United States. Rubén taunts his antagonist: "And I'm sure that if one day the *gringos*[6] decide to take over Panama you will be the first to become a U.S. citizen ... If you're not one already" (p. 193). It is significant to note that when Rubén dies at the very end of the novel, gunned down by a gang of mindless mestizo Panamanian workers in the employ of Fulo Alejandro, it is in Salvador's arms that he breathes his last.

The unrelenting anti*chombo* sentiment is more systematically expressed in the second novel of the trilogy, *Luna verde*. Here it is not really countered by the positive attitudes incorporated into *Curundú* and *Gamboa Road Gang*. *Luna verde's* main protagonist is Ramón de Roquebert, a *latino* Panamanian of rural roots who, under the pressure of socioeconomic forces unleashed by the U.S. occupation, finds himself among the numbers of those swelling the population of Panama City, and inevitably ends up employed on the Canal Zone. Unlike

Rubén, he takes active steps to overcome the gross indignity of being labelled "brown" and being grouped with the *chombos* and others on the "Silver Roll." He sacrifices his personal honor and peace of mind, the honor of his two cousins whom he effectively prostitutes to his two *gringo* bosses, and, of course, the honor and dignity of all of his co-workers. He does not succeed, however, in crossing the color bar into the ranks of the "Gold Roll," and after a serious accident repents his ways, becoming a revolutionary university student. As such, he makes the ultimate sacrifice of his life in a bloody protest against the corruption and shameless capitulation of the national government. The story is told in the first person like *Gamboa Road Gang*, so that the sense of the protagonist as alter ego is even more pronounced.

Luna *verde* has an episodic structure with a whirl of characters who flit across the stage. However, there is a very minor character who, like Red Box, is a forerunner of Atá. He is Michael Deen, known as Sandino. He is a half-East Indian *chombo* (a "dougla") who, like Atá, is tried by the authorities of the Canal Zone and sentenced to an unspeakably harsh prison term for "raping" a white Yankee woman, an ex-night-club girl. In the cryptic style that Beleño employs at times in refreshing contrast to the major-tone apostrophic utterances that abound, he has two chorus-like, unnamed interlocutors sum up the facts of Sandino's tragedy, a poignantly Panamanian one: "She wanted Sandino to promise her marriage so that she could get a divorce from the old *gringo* she had for a husband. Sandino refused. Then, in reprisal, she stole his ID tag and reported him to the Canal Zone police. What would she say to her husband if her child came out black?"[7] The harsh sentence is the white racist response to this assault on their doctrine of inherent superiority, an assault on precisely its most vulnerable and volatile front, namely, the easy access to the supposedly untouchable white woman. Sandino pays fully for his crime of "lese racial superiority." He, like Atá, is gunned down by a prison guard as he attempts an "escape."

Atá is not the main protagonist of *Gamboa Road Gang*, but he is the most important. Like *Luna verde*, the novel is written in the first person, the narrator being a white/mestizo (*latino*) Panamanian who is essentially the same person as Rubén and Ramón, a citizen bitterly aware of his humiliation at the hands of the Yankee invaders who constantly violate in a symbolic and real sense his country, his countrymen, and his countrywomen. The fictional structure is based on this character's imprisonment in the Balboa penitentiary of the Canal Zone along with Atá (Arthur) Ryams and Lester León Greaves. The last named is a personnage taken from real life whose case is echoed in the basic details of Atá's story. Beleño has thereby wedded fact to fiction in an impressively effective manner. The author is thus free to create a character entirely to the specifications of his vision of reality, without divorcing himself entirely from the real world. The fictional aspects invented by Beleño are particularly significant not only artistically but sociologically as well. They manifest the depth of his perception and the shape of it, both being consistent with the general thesis presented in this chapter.

Atá is a special kind of *chombo*, like Red Box, a first generation mulatto, a *negro rubio* (black with blonde hair). His tortured mulatto consciousness will have even more tragic consequences than the madness it produces in Red Box. His *chombo* blood inspires in him too a psychotic hatred for the only group that is willing and eager to accept him. This hatred is symptomatic of a presumed *chombo* inferiority and an equally unscientifically posited Yankee superiority. Like all of Beleño's *chombos* he tends to be servile, and this is reinforced in his case by an absolute contempt for himself and his people. "Yo soy gringo" (I am a *gringo*) is his constant affirmation.

As such, he is entirely within his rights to pursue the fantasy of his relationship with the blue-eyed idol, Annabelle. She, her brother Bobby, and he were childhood playmates when his mother worked as a maid for their family. He meets her again in adulthood during the carnival, and their fleeting moment of mutual fascination culminates in some sort of encounter at night in a lonely spot, the site of their games in the golden days of childhood. To Beleño's artistic credit, it is never clearly established if this encounter amounted to a full sexual act, or whether it was even real and not just a figment of Atá's deranged mulatto mind. The price of life imprisonment is to him a small one to pay for the chimera of his relationship with Annabelle. And certainly all other *chombos* and *chombas* are inconsequential sacrificial lambs to be slaughtered willingly on the altar of this tremendous idol. When Atá, then, directs the following question to the narrator, a fellow inmate of the Gamboa penitentiary, he means it to be merely rethorical: "Chief, you don't believe that a *gringo* like myself ought to sacrifice one of his many little *chombas* for the sake of an amorous correspondence with a *gringa* like Annabelle? Tell me frankly."[8] In prison Atá maintains an extraordinary correspondence with his alleged victim, who speaks of telling the truth and releasing him from his punishment when, in her judgment, he has sufficiently paid for the privilege of her attentions. This situation is perfectly acceptable to Atá, and patently so.

With his servile self-contempt reaching pathological proportions, Atá is very definitely a victim who excites much of the reader's sympathy. He is thereby subsumed fully into the main theme of the novel, and indeed the main concern of the trilogy: bitter protest against the Yankee violation of Panama. In this respect he expiates the *chombo's* general tepidity and enters into Panamanianness as Beleño sees it. For he, like Rubén and Ramón, becomes a full sacrificial lamb forfeiting his life at the hands of the pernicious *gringo* system. In his case the system's murderous machinations are more obvious, direct, and vulgar. Much more so than in the case of Rubén, who is actually killed in defense of his "family land" from which his uncle is being evicted by the new owners, a well-to-do Panamanian family whose wealth is tied to their complicity with the *gringo* invader. Ramón similarly is murdered by Panamanian police and soldiery during the brutal suppression of a student protest against their government's criminal collaboration with the Yankee invader. Atá is, in fact, the direct victim of Yankee violence. He is actually gunned down by a white North-American prison guard at the U.S. Canal Zone penitentiary as he makes a patently suicidal attempt to escape the unjust detention that became an unbearable burden after his fantastic correspondence with Annabelle was terminated and the bundle of letters, the symbol of his aberrantly conceived felicity and hope, disappeared from his cell. Furthermore, since the main protagonist, the first-person narrator, goes on to live more or less happily ever after, the full responsibility of victimhood in the Beleño sense is given to Atá.

Even in his complete victimhood, Atá is not entirely free of the constant stereotypic accusation of complicity with the oppressor. The author has created a complicated symbolism that permits him to wed two contradictory elements: Atá as victim of the invader, like the Panamanian par excellence, and Atá as the enemy's servile ally, a traitor to the Panamanian cause. Atá is a *chombo blanco*, a *negro rubio*, a "red," a mulatto, or half-breed. He is an *"enrazado,"* and the author gives a clear definition of this term: "Every *enrazado* is a *gringo* imprisoned in a black jail and a nappy head. ... And so the arrogant *gringo* is reduced to the black backyard and black life-style" (p. 173). The jail imagery is of course particularly apt, but the terms in which the idea is presented are the usual ones of anti-*chombo* prejudice predicated on the assumption of black inferiority. Considering himself a *gringo* with primordial cultural and political allegiance to the U.S. system and despising non*gringos*, especially *chombos*, Atá is the perfect scapegoat for all groups. It is through his depiction of the resentment fellow West Indians feel towards Atá that Beleño gives full and explicit expression to the symbolism, a twist of particularly cruel irony. The first-person narrator in the following passage explains:

> In my view, the hatred expressed by Wallai [a West Indian fellow prisoner] was towards Atá the *gringo* prisoner and not towards that other Atá, the son of Nelly from Loma de San Miguel. If some blond man had been sitting there Wallai would not dare to have told him such hurtful things, but one could say such things to Atá because it was not the *chombo* but the *gringo* that was being insulted. He was taking revenge on the poor defenseless *gringo* who was slowly dying in Atá. (p. 197)

This view of things apparently is satisfactory to all, except of course the poor *"enrazado."* However, upon careful consideration it is hardly acceptable to the West Indians either. For all the sympathy that the author extends to Atá and has him evoke in the reader, the odious prejudice, the automatic rejection syndrome is also manifest.

All in all, the interplay of the contradictory approaches to West Indians has helped Beleño's art, especially in the matter of Atá's characterization. For he is, indeed, "the most real and complete" of his characters. The West Indian presence then provides one of the most important stimuli to Beleño's creativity in these three novels which constitute the major part of his work.[9]

Two Views from the Outside

Demetrio Aguilera Malta

It can be affirmed then that what I have termed "the view from beneath the bed" accounts for Beleño's success in the portrayal of West Indian characters. My research appears to corroborate the corrollary of this assertion: in so far as the other non-West Indian authors are not able to adopt a viewing stance similar to the young Rubén's, they fail in their portrayal of West Indian life and characters. The novel *Canal Zone* by the Ecuadorian Demetrio Aguilera Malta is a case in point. First published in 1935, it clearly predates all of the other Central American literature in Spanish that deals with the West Indian theme. In fact, the main character, Pedro Coorsi, is a *chombo* of the same racial mix as Red Box and Atá, that is, he is the offspring of a black West Indian mother and a white father. To be more specific, Pedro's father is a Greek worker. Thus Pedro is not only the first important West Indian character in Hispanic Central American literature, but he is the only West Indian main chracter to appear in any of this literature written by non-West Indians.

However, Pedro does not really perceive himself to be *chombo*. Everybody else does, but nowhere in the novel is he made to give evidence of any clear and real consciousness of belonging to a group that is culturally and socioeconomically distinct from the Panamanian mainstream group. Even at the climactic moment of his death the idea that he fixates on is that of the woe that afflicts the nation as a whole, the problem of the Canal. This sense of being other than a member of the only group he can realistically belong to may have been created by the author to heighten Pedro's existential alienation. For somewhat like a William Faulkner character, or a Meursault (of Albert Camus's *L'Etranger*), Pedro never seems to integrate himself fully into the rhythm of his own existence. He drifts from situation to situation until he finally meets his death as a result of a possibly suicidal automobile accident when, in a distracted fit of reflection on the monumental injustice of things, his car collides with a pole. If indeed Aguilera Malta did set out to create an existential hero then he missed the chance to create as well an authentic Panamanian one.

In the early stages of the novel, for example, Pedro is laid off from his job with his boss adducing the general reason of "la crisis" (the crisis).[10] However, Pedro is the only one in his immediate gang to be fired, even the other *chombos*, because of their seniority, keep their jobs for the time being. This clearly indicates that the boss considered him a common or garden *chombo*. Certainly this must have been a shock to the character who was presented deliberately, or apparently so, by the author as not quite aware of his "chomboness." This situation is thus full of the dramatic tension of the problem of identity. Not only does Aguilera Malta choose to ignore the artistic potential of this particular problem, but he also fails to explore the manifestly rich potential of the related question of *mestizaje* and mulatto identity. Time and time again he tantalizes the reader by exposing Pedro to situations that cry out for full penetration into the complexities of the mulatto consciousness. Pedro's friends from high school all seem to be white/mestizo Eurocentric Panamanians of the middle class, and on his occasional outings with them Pedro does not quite fit in. However, the author simply glosses over this circumstance.

West Indians are portrayed in very few dimensions, the major focus being on the socioeconomic process, for example, the landlord/tenant relationship. Thus the rent strike led by West Indians is a significant part of the action of the book. The author focuses too on the employer/employee relationship. Hence we see Pedro moving from his job at the newspaper press to a long period of joblessness that occupies the larger part of the novel, and thence to his demeaning job as a taxi driver ferrying U.S. servicemen to Tommy's house of sophisticated prostitution. We also see the hardships of *chomba* women who wash clothes for a living. Apart from these socioeconomic relationships, the author turns his attention occasionally to casual sexual encounters. Absent is any serious concentration on the intimate interpersonal relations among West Indians. Absent too is any consideration of their religiousness or their peculiar linguistic situation. All of these areas would have afforded Aguilera Malta a better opportunity for real penetration into the *chombo* ethos.

Of course, all of the usual stereotypes are present in the author's portrayal of *chombo* life and culture. The most flamboyant is the *chombo's* proclivity for sex and dance. It must be said though that, for the author, lasciviousness is not the exclusive province of West Indians, for the novel is full of sexual cavorting engaged in indiscriminately by all groups. The most disturbing of the stereotypes, one that is repeatedly aired in works of Beleño and all the other non-West Indians, is the West Indian's fatalistic acceptance of his inferior status, and of the injustices perpetrated against him. This is very clearly depicted in the following words referring to Pedro's *chomba* mother: "She thought of her son. She imagined him struggling desperately and always losing. It was fate ... She had always seen it in all the men of her race. It was of no use that her son carried that little bit of white blood."[11] The mother's negativism will turn out to be prophetic, self-fulfillingly so.

The resulting work is consequently annoyingly superficial. While Pedro, the son of a *chomba*, is the main character, he is a mere shadow compared to Red Box, not to mention Atá. The differential factor at the creative level can be reduced to the absence in Canal Zone of "the view from beneath the bed."

Carlos Luis Fallas

Wearing the cap of the literary historian, Quince Duncan has written on"El negro en la literatura costarricense"[12] (Blacks in Costa Rican Literature). He refers to the following works as having some kind of black presence: *Mamita Yunai* and *Gentes y gentecillas* by Carlos Luis Fallas; *Puerto Limón, Manglar, Murámonos Federico*, and *Cocorí* by Joaquín Gutiérrez *La isla de los hombres solos, Picahueso,* and "Una guitarra para José de Jesús" by José León Sánchez; "El jaspe," "La mujer negra del Río,"and"El gato con botas" by Fabián Dobles; *Más abajo de la piel* by Abel Pacheco; and, of course, the works by Duncan himself. According to Duncan's own analysis the black presence is minimal in many of these works cited. I feel that Carlos Luis Fallas's *Mamita Yunai* (1941), and Joaquín Gutiérrez' *Puerto Limón* (1950) are indeed the pioneering works that put Costa Rican West Indians solidly on the literary map for the first time. Abel Pacheco's work is more fully West Indian than any of the works produced by any of the other *latino* Costa Ricans. However, appearing in 1972, his *Más abajo de la piel* cannot be considered a pioneering production.

Fallas's work, in a direct, unpolished, openly autobiographical, first-person narrative tells of his experiences in the province of Limón during two different periods separated by fourteen years. The first (it is chronologically the second) covers his experience during a farcically irregular election process that he attempts to monitor, the second, his experiences as a young man of nineteen years working as a semiskilled laborer for the United Fruit Company.

In spite of the testimonial nature of the work, Fallas's contact with West Indians is extremely limited. He views them from the outside, with some sympathy but with much of the automatic prejudice. This becomes clear in the very opening scene of the novel. On a train on his way from the central high-valley region down into the coastal tropical Limón province, the author describes his exposure to West Indians: "The majority of the passengers were young people of the colored race"[13] He finds himself immersed in a "mare-magnum de inglés y español" (noisy confusion of English and Spanish) (p. 16). It turns out that these West Indians are part of the large groups that, consequent on the closing down of the United Fruit Company's operations on the Atlantic coast during the thirties, were forced to leave their homes to go to Panama to find work. (They were prohibited by a law promulgated on December 10, 1934 from moving to the Pacific coast to seek work on the Company's new installations there).[14] The author is sensitive to the historical reality, and, in this spirit of fidelity to the facts, the West Indians make their appearance. They are not, however, essential to the action.

The high point of this opening scene is attained in the following paragraph:

> It would seem that for these black people the wheels of history had stopped, that as far as they were concerned the French Revolution had still not blossomed, Lincoln had not existed, nor had Bolivar waged his struggles, nor had the black Maceo covered himself in glory. And now these Costa Rican blacks, after having enriched the banana barons with their blood, had to flee by night across the mountains, dragging their children and their belongings with them. It wasn't the slavers' dog that was chasing them, it was rather the specter of poverty. (p. 26)

Such lines could only be penned by a sensitive man knowledgeable about

Western economic history and aware of the black man's role in that history. In Duncan's view Fallas "discovered the epic dimension of the facts and produced one of the most beautiful pages ever written on blacks by any Costa Rica."[15] The beauty springs principally from the prose style, which is, according to Duncan, ". . . A mixture of lyricism and of history, politics and protest" (p. 15). However, the vision Fallas presents is definitely not developed beneath the bed." He remains simply a white/mestizo Costa Rican sharing a train ride with some disadvantaged West Indians with whom he can empathize.

The "otherness" of blacks is reconfirmed through the book especially in the second half. The scene in which the author/observer sets out to describe how blacks spent *their* leisure time on Saturday nights out in the wilderness work camps of the United Fruit Company opens in the following manner: "the black workers lived in the camp opposite. They too were hanging out in their open corredors" (p. 133). The terms of reference are clearly set up, the "them vs us" relationship, the separate but supposedly equal situation accepted as perfectly "natural" in spite of the special circumstances of isolation and labor out there in the inhospitable jungle and in spite, too, of occasional interracial friendships.

Throughout the scene the author is undoubtedly sympathetic, understanding his socioeconomic solidarity with black workers and recognizing their common plight as victims of the same exploiters. (This is significant since the novel does contain a scene [p. 50] in which a black clerk in a Company store is presented as a co-exploiter in the manner in which Beleno presents the petty black functionaries on the Canal Zone). Fallas even dispels, during the course of the passage under consideration, one of the myths about blacks, resolutely affirming: "They are strong and enduring in work" (p. 134). However, many of the usual prejudices persist. For example, in describing a game of dominos, a regular leisure time activity for the black workers, he has them slamming the dominos against the board "*con fuerza bestial*" (with bestial force) (p. 133). The ensuing discussions and arguments are described thus: "And they would argue shouting horribly and gesticulating like devils; anyone would think that they were about to kill each other." When they sang they, of course, "would sing in English, in call/response pattern, a savage monotonous song" (p. 134). On the basis of his fundamental ignorance—he speaks no English—he makes the judgment about the monotony and savagery of the song. Their dance is seen along the same lines: "One performed dizzying footwork doing unbelievable things with his feet. Another disjointed his waist in an obscene and libidinous dance" (p. 135). To make matters perfectly clear, after this two and one-half page section describing how the blacks spent their leisure hours, the author begins the next section with the words: "*We* also would get drunk from time to time" (p. 136, emphasis added). He then goes on to describe how *their* drunkenness differed from that of the blacks.

Joaquín Gutiérrez: Half In, Half Out

In contrast to Fallas, the author of *Puerto Limón* is a native of the province of Limón and consequently grew up in physical proximity to West Indians. The deeper knowledge resulting from this exposure has enabled him partially to achieve the "view from beneath the bed." Whereas Fallas is singularly lacking in the creation of any West Indian character, Gutiérrez has managed to take his art beyond mere anthropological style observation to the point of fully including the West Indian experience into his sphere of creativity. His most successful effort in this regard is the character Tom Winkelman. Duncan is much pleased with this character: "But Tom is indeed a black man from Limón in the fullest sense. In other words, Gutiérrez in Tom has created his best black character. He has all the cultural features of the Afro-Caribbean" (p. 20). So successful is Gutiérrez' characterization that Duncan makes the impressive claim that Tom "reminds us of many a black man we used to know in our infancy. A pensive, confused man, a victim of his reality..." (p. 22). The other West Indian character Azucena, Tom's sister, is not in Duncan's opinion such a successful creation: "One gets the impression that she was a black woman that the author had loved greatly—perhaps while still a boy—and who had disappeared from the scene before he could understand her" (p. 20). The author's failures with Azucena have to be weighed against his successes with Tom in order to appreciate fully his capacity to create fiction.

Azucena fails as a character because the general and the stereotypic overview of West Indians interfered with the author's perception of the individual. The most offensive stereotype in the portrayal of Azucena is that of the Negro as child—particularly ironic in view of our theory. It is tempting to theorize, and Duncan's analysis would invite such speculation, that Gutiérrez the white/mestizo child was unable to get beneath the bed since as a member of the upper class his view of blacks like Azucena would have been from the veranda, that is, down upon, with the consequent limiting trajectory, rather than up and out, with the consequent expanding trajectory. The intimacy achieved would be one that was regulated and ordained by the class relationship, not the natural spontaneous openness. As such, the vision would be profoundly affected by the dictates of automatic prejudice and stereotype; the most pertinent one for the child would be precisely, the Negro as child. The facts of the plot seer.ı to bear out this analysis. Silvano, the main protagonist, and presumably the author's alter ego, is the newphew/son of a wealthy white landowner from the Limón province. The story is set during the mid-thirties, the time of the historic strike against the United Fruit Company. Silvano is an existentialist hero: a young man struggling principally to find some meaning to his existence, relentlessly dogged by a vague but real malaise. Azucena is the faithful household maid; Tom, her brother, is a black worker of a certain rank, for he drives the Company motor car. He is not in the employ of Silvano's family, and this is significant.

Sympathetic as Silvano and indeed his family are towards Azucena, it is a sympathy based on her inferior status—not unlike the sympathy and kindness a master would extend to a faithful slave. The patronizing goodwill sinks to an infamous low on the occasion when Azucena, who had been complaining of a strange numbness in her extremities, is granted time off to see the master's family doctor. The latter invites the teenage Silvano to accompany his uncle into the examining room, to have a look for themselves at the middle-aged black woman patient. This would have been appropriate if Azucena were the family pet, or a small child. To make matters worse, her upper thighs are exposed because this is the area to which the doctor had been directing his professional attentions. The psychology of the white ruling class is clearly exposed in these words the doctor uses to calm Azucena's legitimate although limply expressed protest: "Why are you ashamed? Didn't they themselves send you here to be cured?"[16] And to roundly established the idea of Azucena as child, Gutiérrez unsubtly presents the image of the doctor who, not wanting to alarm his patient, spells out the word leprosy to the white guests/spectators, who thereby become the first to know of the middle-aged black woman's condition: "The doctor turned them to the Rojases and told them, spelling out the word L - e - p - r - o - s - y." Indeed the author has Azucena utter twice the muted protest, "Oh Lord, what a shame, what a shame!" (p. 90). Frankly, however, the reader is left with the distinct impression that the fictional white men, as well as the author himself, miss the profound significance of Azucena's utterance.

In his relationship with Tom, Silvano manifests some degree of the natural spontaneity and openness not so totally affected by the mechanical attitudes imposed by the master-servant, employer-employee situation. In fact, one finds a similar level of openness in Silvano's relationship with Tom as in Rubén's with Tamtam and Liequí (in Beleño's *Curundú*). Silvano can admire and respect Tom's manhood while he is quite cognizant of his victimhood. This subtle combination of admiration and sympathy is the basis of the author's authenticity in the creation of Tom's character. This is why Tom, in Duncan's judgement, is such a real person. The author's dramatic skills have created at least one scene in which, through the mechanism of his art, he displays all of Tom's endearing "old-time" West Indian qualities that Duncan spoke about. In it Tom explodes into a desperate reaction to the dark cloud of frustration and constant sense of exploitation under which he lives. He runs the Company's expensive motor car at full speed into the end of the line, which, acting like a trampoline, hurtles the car and its occupant through the air into the sea. The dramatic act of rebellion with the suicidal risk it involves elicits the thunderous applause of all. Tom's seminaive display of "hombría" (manhood) reminds us of the adolescent strutting form of manhood exhibited by Liequí and Tamtam, which Rubén found so attractive.

There is a deeper significance to Tom's act which connects it more intimately to the main action. In the first instance this act of suicidal recklessness is juxtaposed to Silvano's existential meditation on the desirability of suicide. Secondly, it is clearly inspired by Tom's childish sense of wondrous admiration at an analogous experience Silvano had had when his bicycle, going at full speed, got caught on the curb as he attempted to avoid a passing cow, with the result that he was hurtled through the air above the rails and onto the floor of an open veranda in a nearby house. Tom's reaction to the recounting of the incident is: "Oh, what a jump, Jesus Christ, what a jump!" (p. 42). Silvano's experience makes an indelible impression on Tom's mind—the inference of childishness has to be drawn. Furthermore, Silvano related this incident to Tom on the occasion on which his uncle "railroaded" the black employee into risking his job by giving them a ride in the **Company** motor car. Tom, consistent with his quality of dashing, carefree "manhood," drove the car on that occasion at a recklessly rapid pace. However, just as Silvano's childhood experience prefigured Tom's "manly" act of rebellion, this very act turned out to prefigure the final tragic scene. The book ends with the unfortunate death of Silvano's uncle, Don Hector, and the Nicaraguan strike leader, Paraguitas, who, just after making their reconciliation, plunge off a broken bridge in their speeding motor car. These threads of interconnection add to Tom's stature as a character in the novel, and thereby eloquently testify to the significance of West Indian life and culture in Guitérrez' creativity.

Duncan's fine combing of Costa Rican literature for any traces of black presence has turned up some mention of blacks in two novels by Gutiérrez: *Manglar* (1947), and *Murámonos Federico* (1973). Neither work has anything to do, in any real sense, with black people—West Indians in the Costa Rican setting. Their presence is reduced to a mere mention indeed: one that would only be of significance to readers who were either totally ignorant or possessed of the vaguest notions about the geographical confines of African cultural influence.

An early work by Gutiérrez, *Cocorí* (1948), is substantially and, in fact, exclusively dedicated to the portrayal of "black" life. Since, however, these black people are non-West Indian, they have to be an abstraction given the Costa Rican reality such as was alluded to in the Introduction. Duncan dismisses the work as a depiction of black life precisely on the basis of the critical question of characterization: "*Cocorí* the little black boy, the Black Singer, and Mama Drusila could just as well have been Chinese without any effect on the moral of the work."[17]

It is somewhat ironic but not entirely surprising that an author such as Guitérrez should attain his highest commercial success with a work such as *Cocorí*, involving the creation of a main character who is both black and a child. If his entire creative effort had been more fully informed by the child's "view from beneath the bed," his adult black characters would have been perhaps more artistically successful, less tainted with the fossilized Negro-as-child approach.

There are yet other non-West Indian Costa Ricans whose literary use of the theme of West Indian life and culture preceded the full flowering of a West Indian literature in that country. Fabián Dobles, for instance, created an *antillano* principal character, Sammy (Sam Scott), in his short story, *El jaspe* (1956). Yet another short story, "El gato con zapatos," from the collection, *Historias de Tata Mundo* (1955), also set on the banana plantations of the province of Limón, provides some very minor West Indian characters.[18] Duncan is perfectly correct when he judges Dobles's contribution to be more in the realm of ideology than literary creativity. He asserts that "What interests Fabián Dobles are not the cultural differences" (p. 16). These would have provided a solid basis for artful characterization. However, Dobles prefers to focus on elements that appeal more directly to the intellectual rather than the artistic man, principally the concept of racial harmony and intergroup understanding.

Substantially the same judgment is passed on the works of José León Sánchez. The closest he comes to creating a West Indian character is in his short story, or rather short-story length prison narrative, entitled "Una guitarra para José de Jesús" (actually written in 1959 while he was incarcerated in the Presidio de San Lucas). The character is Mister Smith, "... un negro de Limón" (a black man from Limon).[19] In fact, José de Jesús is also black, but the blackness of both of these characters is incidental to the main action and the very meaning of the story. It is a drama of incarceration. To quote Duncan, "... Black people in Sánchez narrative are not really Limón blacks ... Afro-Caribbeans. In no way does their behaviour differ from that of any other *afrolatindigena*" (p. 18).

The Influence

Language

The influence exerted by West Indian life and culture has been significant, not only in the area of characterization but in other structural aspects of contemporary Hispanic Central American literature. One such aspect is the linguistic. There is, in fact, a close correlation between the different levels of authenticity achieved by the different authors in the portrayal of *antillano* characters and the level of familiarity with the special linguistic situation of the West Indian group. Beleño and Gutiérrez, the two most artistically successful of the "precursors," are also the ones who have most successfully handled this linguistic material. Aguilera Malta, whose treatment of *chombos* was seen to be manifestly superficial, understandably made no attempt to incorporate the matter of *chombo* speech into his creativity. In between these two extremes the other authors can be placed in strict correlation to their efforts at characterization. Chapter Two will study fully the question of the use of language not only by the non-West Indian precursors but also by the new West Indian authors themselves.

Themes: The Plantation, Interracial Love, Mestizaje, Religion, and Carnival

The study of the works of the precursors has unearthed the fact that there are certain patterns in the modes employed in the presentation of West Indian life and culture. The modes of conceiving the culture can be considered best in the light of the themes that tend to be predomiant in the creative works. Just as the use of Afro-Caribbean speech points the way towards the new West Indian literature, so too do these recurrent themes which touch on the essence of West Indian life and culture, and which, as well, affect the basic structure of the novels, poems, and short stories under consideration. The themes that I have chosen as basic are, then, more than mere motifs, they have to do with the structural underpinnings of the writers' view of the world, and perhpas mirror the West Indian way of seeing the world.

West Indian life and culture are presented in all of the works, without exception, as intimately and inextricably bound up with the political and socioeconomic forces in the society. One could even speak of the "plantation model" as the basis on which the various fictional universes in these various works have been created. Thus the West Indian characters are never seen except in their relationships, sometimes intimate and profound, sometimes more superficial, to the plantation—the plantation as it evolved in the Central American situation. This new plantation can be reduced to two essential elements: the company, the commercial entity, and the "zone" or the traditional plantation, the physical entity. The entire life experience of the Central American West Indian is circumscribed within the limits of these two elements. In Panama, the Panama Canal Company and the Canal Zone are the constituent elements of the paradigm, whereas in Costa Rica the corresponding elements are basically the United Fruit Company and the banana plantations.[20] The situation of West Indians elicits cries of protest from the various authors, and this protest itself with all of its elements and ramifications becomes a theme.

Although Beleño's "chombos" (in Curundú, Luna verde, and Gamboa Road Gang) have no validity apart from the Panama Canal Company and the Zone, the sense of protest and profound outrage that Beleño evokes is not chombo-centered but rather latino-centered. In fact, as the study of his use of characterization revealed, over and over again Panamanians of Anglophone Caribbean background are presented partially as associates of the Yankee "masters," self-destructively collaborating in the process of oppression.

A similar ambivalence consequent on the polarity between the author and the West Indian group is seen in Fallas. He has a scene in Mamita Yunai in which a petty functionary of the Company's commissary lords it over the white/mestizo protagonist and his buddies, practising the petty viciousness that oppressed people are wont to visit upon their fellow sufferers. The protagonist/author and his friends seeth with a particular rage at the indignity suffered at the hands of this black "inferior." With the directness of style that characterizes the novel, the author sums up the reaction as follows: "We left the commissary cursing the black man, the policeman and the United" (p. 158). The novel itself contains an appendix which consists of an entire speech given by Fallas in his capacity as a labor leader. In it he affirms: "The Company in order to guard against the possibility of serious rebellions, stirred up feelings of hatred of whites for blacks and blacks for whites, and they were successful" (p. 197). This confirms the reader's suspicions that the deep underlying resentment and antipathy towards West Indians were reflections of the real feelings of the author and his peers.

In Gutierrez' Tom Winkleman (of *Puerto Limón*) there is, as well, a hint of cowardly complicity with the enemy. Tom does not participate in the strike, and the author suggests that his narrow self-interest could frustrate the general efforts for the common good. However, because the author's perspective is non-West Indian—and indeed it is not that of the *latino* oppressed class either—this aspect of the theme is not allowed to develop. Gutiérrez presentation is consequently somewhat more finely chiselled than either Beleño's or Fallas's, for the concept of the plantation is more subtly elaborated. The class relationships are not merely those of the national and seminational oppressed to the international capitalist oppressor, but the "national bourgeoisie," the true co-oppressor class, is treated as the center of focus. Silvano the protagonist and alter ego of the author is a son of the national bourgeoisie. So that, if not Tom, at least his sister Azucena is the direct victim of the national bourgeois class, and her plantation takes the form of the "big house" and the master-servant relationship. Tom, however, the most complete West Indian character, can certainly be defined solidly in terms of the basic plantation model that I have presented. He is an employee of the United Fruit Company, an exploited one whose revolt was discussed earlier.

In Aguilera Malta's *Canal Zone*, as the very title indicates, the fictional universe is essentially a function of political and socioeconomic forces, the characters being presented solely in terms of the ensuing relationships. The dedication of the book reads: "I dedicate this book to the black people of Chorrillo and Calidonia. To Panama's revolutionary mestizos and whites. To the automatized sailors of the American fleet." In this accomodationist perspective, the West Indians are not the only victims, and the concept of their complicity with the oppressor is necessarily absent. Pedro, the half-*chombo* main character is ground to death by the infernal machine of the plantation system, and the book consists of the presentation of the various phases and forms of this process as it affects not only Pedro but all the members of the groups mentioned in the dedication. (The author is obviously stretching the plantation concept to its furthest limits). The author's note of protest reaches its climax at the end of the novel with Pedro's death in absolute and total abandonment and haunted by the oppressive specter of the Zone. The final words he utters are: "—El Canal ..." (p. 154), the sole words to escape his lips during his final agony, and the words with which Aguilera Malta dramatically concludes the novel.

A similar level of idealism unaccompanied by any solid demonstration of familiarity with the reality of Afro-Caribbean life and culture marks the approach of authors like Fabián Dobles and José León Sánchez. They present West Indians essentially in terms of their relationship to the plantation—the plantation in the strictest sense enshrined in our presentation of the model. This relationship, as is the case with Aguilera Malta, is one-dimensional.

The new West Indian authors will continue this socioeconomic focus. However, their approach will be completely Afro-Caribbean, free of the hostility and ambivalence toward West Indians of a Fallas or a Beleño. This springs not from deliberate avoidance nor ignorance but from a complete identity with the West Indian, and a profound understanding of the world as he sees it. A most striking demonstration of this kind of understanding and identification is to be found, for example, in Abel Pacheco's *Más abajo de la piel* (1972), a work, by a nonblack Caribbean author, which could be considered legitimately part of the body of contemporary West Indian literature from Costa Rica.[21] The book is a collection of prose poems in the first of which the author establishes his focus.

The black man was not brought here, he was called and he came
The swamp that had swallowed up the Indian, the Creole, the Italian,
the Chinaman respected the immense black man.[22]

Not all of the poems are about Afro-Caribbean people, but the majority are. Many present West Indians in their essential relationship to the plantation in its basic acceptation. "Papa Uriah" and "Sin echar raices," for example, refresh the reader's memory on the circumstances of the Afro-Caribbean people's initial migration to Costa Rica. "La garantía de un contrato," and "Sigatoka y similares" speak of specific injustices of the plantation system. In the latter the Company unconscionably evicts West Indians from the land carved out with their sweat and blood, so that "Now there are banana fields where the cocoa once grew" (p. 40).

The theme of the plantation and the consequent social protest colors the prose and poetry of Cubena. It is present in the poetry of both Gerardo Maloney and Eulalia Bernard, and is one of the artistic pillars of Quince Duncan's fictional universe, in such works as "La rebelión pocomía" and *La paz del pueblo*, which will be studied later.

The plantation is one of the most important of the socioeconomic structures generated by colonialism, and as Frantz Fanon astutely pointed out, the colonial world is essentially "Manichean."[23] Fortunately, man always tends towards an equilibrium often achieved in spite of himself because of his fundamental thrust towards contradiction. So the polarization of peoples, races, classes, or groups has historically simply been one part of an overall process, a dialectic. In these terms, the thesis of separation has generated the antithesis of intergroup unions on an individual basis and against all the prevailing laws, customs, mores, and taboos. This has lead to the inevitable synthesis. The process is evident wherever the infernal machine of colonization in any one of its multiple forms has been at work. In the Americas and elsewhere, where the plantation has imposed the logic of racism and apartheid, interracial sex has been the natural antithesis that results in the synthesis of *mestizaje*.[24] Thus the themes of interracial love and *mestizaje* are fundamental themes in Afro-Spanish American literature,[25] or in Euro-Spanish American literature that may include the black presence. Examples of the former case are found in Adalberto Ortiz's *Juyungo*, Ramón Díaz Sánchez' *Cumboto*, Manuel Zapata Oliveilla's *Chambacú, corral de negros*, Nelson Estupiñán Bass's *El último río*, or the vast majority of the West Indian works that this book will study. Rómulo Gallegos' *Pobre negro* is a good example of the latter type, as are the majority of the non-West Indian works studied in this book.

Beleño's *Atá*, from *Gamboa Road Gang*, and his predecessor Sandino, from *Luna verde*, are concretizations of the theme of interracial sex and its corrollary, *mestizaje*. Pedro from *Canal Zone* is also smitten with a problematic fascination for a white/mestizo woman, Violeta Lunares. She is presented in typical fashion as the forbidden fruit intensely craved by the black character, and who is either materially unattainable, as is the case with Pedro, or who can be obtained only at the cost of immense labor and at the risk of unspeakable punishment even death, as is the case with Atá and Sandino. Joaquín Gutiérrez in *Cocorí* presents what can be seen as a variation on the theme that is more apt for a young audience. Fallas, Dobles, and León Sánchez avoid the theme.

It is noteworthy that whereas the West Indian and other black authors in general have indeed depicted an intense preoccupation with white women on the part of their black male characters, it is not the one-sided neurosis that non-West Indian and nonblack authors have painted. Most importantly, the white woman is not seen as some unreal treasure, unattainable or barely attainable, but rather as a quite accessible sexual companion. The problem lies not in gaining the favors of a white consort, but in reconciling the ensuing relationship with the realities of day to day life in a racist society. Charles McForbes, the protagonist in Duncan's *Los cuatro espejos* marries a white woman from the capital city's high-class society, and this leads to his acute identity crisis which is the main element of the plot. Cubena's cosmopolitan alter ego moves in the upper circles of the international professional class, and whether he takes the form of Dr. Cubena—in "La depravada"—or Cubena —the young Los Angeles based Panamanian writer in "La fiesta" — the interracial sexual relationship is an accepted part of his reality.[26] However, it is fraught with sociological and psychological problems. Cubena the poet, in *Pensamientos del negro Cubena*, sings to muses of various hues and colors. His is not the tortured cry of a would-be lover, but the love song of one who has loved and been loved in return. Pacheco in his very West Indian work does not treat the theme, nor do Gerardo Maloney and Eulalia Bernard in the works that have appeared so far.

Significantly Beleño's and, to a lesser degree, Aguilera Malta's concern with the problem of the mulatto is not developed by any of the West

Indian writers. This is one of the most impressive differences between the new Central American black literature and the corpus of Afro-Spanish American literature. The latter has largely focussed on the mulatto, seeing *mestizaje* as the major force and shaping element in race relations. Such a perspective, of course, is not entirely consistent with the sense of self-worth and the racial pride of Latin America's black population. The approach of Duncan, Cubena, and Maloney is thus one that is more integrally black, presenting a perspective on race relations with which countless millions of black peoples in the Americas and elsewhere can instinctively identify.

Anthropologists have generally claimed that African culture is religious-oriented. By extension the religious focus would be basic to the presentation of West Indian life and culture. Beleño shows some sense of appreciating this principle, for his chief West Indian character in his chronologically first novel, *Curundú*, is Salvador Brown, a fanatical young lay minister of a minor Christian sect. His ideological confrontation with the main character, Rubén's, catholicism is meant to be a principal element of the plot, for it is constant, and the two characters are equal in every respect except for their religion and their race. Salvador's officious proselytizing certainly reflects one style of Afro-Caribbean religiousity.

By this measure most of the other non-West Indian authors have failed to capture the essence of West Indian life, for they have missed the centrality of the religious theme. Pacheco fully understands West Indian religiousness, and is sensitive to its aesthetic importance. In fact, he may err on the side of excessive concern with the exotic aspects. For example, in "Misa," his celebration of the folk ritual contains some exotic, jungle, and, even erotic elements. Duncan is entirely above either the occasional unbalanced prurience of Pacheco's approach, or the touches of bitter scepticism of the early Cubena and Bernard, as will be seen in Chapters Four and Five. Maloney's published work is still not voluminous enough to provide any firm assessment of his approach to the theme of religion.

Carnival is, in a real sense, central to Caribbean culture, being an activity that combines many of the secularly important threads of this culture, both the directly and indirectly religious. Many non-West Indians and even West Indians fail to recognize the centrality of carnival. However, Beleno's most important and complete West Indian character, Atá, is a calypsonian. The central action of the plot of *Gamboa Road Gang* takes place during carnival, and it is through the medium of the calypso that Atá most completely expresses his sentiments for Annabelle:

> Annabelle ... Annabelle
> You go to heaven
> And me go to hell. (p. 99)

Beleño fully understands that the calypso, the carnival song par excellence, is one of the most significant African elements of Caribbean culture. He describes calypsoes as having "a strange West Indian sadness, similar to those tyrannical and stimulating Gospel songs that try to hide a God still not fully unearthed from the African jungles" (p. 122). The moment of truth, when the author asserts that "For the first time during the entire period that he had spent in prison, Atá the white black man accepted the fact of his being black," is followed by an action that must be seen as profoundly significant. "Right then Atá made up a swing-calypso which speaks of two parallel lines that converge at death, of a black soul and a white one moving towards infinity" (p. 149). The symbol of the parallel lines and the message of the song are fundamentally insightful and indeed prophetic. Calypso singing is, then, not just an idle pastime, it is a poetic act in the fullest sense of the term. Thus at the very end of the work, on what is effectively the final page, the central calypso is repeated by the author in final tribute to Atá, and as a magical formula which contains the essence, material and immaterial, of the plot:

Annabelle ... Annabelle
You go to heaven
And me go to hell (p. 218)

Carnival in Aguilera Malta's *Canal Zone* is less noble, it is a touristically viewed black ritual of atavistic primitivism in which the erotic predominates. However, at least the author glimpsed the centrality of the festival and captured its sense as a fertility rite, and a national catharsis.

Cubena is ill at ease with this aspect of West Indian life. His carnivals, like the more direct manifestations of African religious traditions, tend to be seen as distractions. (This point will be further discussed in Chapter Four). Bernard has a somewhat less negative view of carnival, and neither Duncan nor Maloney has devoted much time to the exploration of this theme. The experience of the other Caribbean literatures suggests that the calypso like the Cuban *son*, for example, can be a significant source of inspiration for the Central American poets for whom the calypso is an item of cultural heritage.[27] However, as Chapter Five will indicate this vision of things has so far generally escaped the West Indian Central American poets.

The non-West Indian precursors have, then, indeed taken the lead in developing some of the important themes that touch on the essence of West Indian life and culture. However, the world view that has evolved, even with these keen insights, is not coherently and fundamentally West Indian. This was seen to be the case in the matter of the depiction of characters, in the use of Afro-Caribbean speech, as well as in the question of thematic content. All in all then, in important aspects of form and content it can be asserted that the precursors blazed a trail that the younger West Indian writers could use effectively and expand upon.

The rest of this book will attempt to expose to the reader's view a clear picture of the organically structured, intrinsically West Indian, fictional universes created by the new Afro-Caribbean writers, using the same basic elements employed by the non*antillano* predecessors. The idea of language as one of the bases of the West Indian world view will be examined, showing how language is organically integrated into the whole picture. For this aspect Duncan's and Cubena's fictional universes will be the precise object of our attention. By applying essentially to them the same terms of analysis we hope to highlight the coherently West Indian nature of their respective works. In both cases we have tried to discover some central axis around which the coherence is structured. With Duncan, Afro-Caribbean religious tradition constitutes the central axis. In the case of Cubena, it is the sense of the selfhood of the entire Afro-Antillean people. We have studied Maloney and Bernard in the context of the bourgeoning Central American West Indian poetry, and, consistent with the general lines established in the preceding pages of the book, we have attempted to identify the core West Indian features of this new poetry. The conclusion will simply essay a glimpse into the future.

CHAPTER TWO

THE LANGUAGE OF THE NEW WEST INDIAN LITERATURE

... sentez-vous cette souffrance
Et ce désespoir à nul autre égal
D'apprivoiser, avec des mots de France,
Ce coeur qui m'est venu du Sénégal?

Léon Laleau

It was pointed out in the Introduction that West Indians in Panama, Costa Rica, Nicaragua, and the other Central American nations, constitute an ethnolinguistic minority group. Their native language, or that of their immediate ancestors, is the axis around which their relationships with all other groups in the nation revolve.[1] Indeed, it is a factor that touches on the essence of their being, affecting every sphere of existence and, most importantly, their very self-concept. The Ramirez, III theory, presented in the Introduction, represents one way of approaching the rich gamut of possibilities for the individual of an ethnolinguistic minority group to relate to the society in which he finds himself. The study of these phenomena is a fertile field for the sociolinguist, the psycholinguist, the sociologist, the psychologist, the anthropologist, and indeed for any other researcher in any one of the many branches of social or behavioral sciences and studies. It seems clear, however, that literature, the highest and most intense cultural use of language, will be the area of research most relevant to the study of ethnolinguistic minority groups. Furthermore, the exclusive linguistic aspects of literary analysis should be even more pertinent to any such study. This present chapter is, then, of pivotal importance. It will show how the question of language impinges upon the creativity of West Indian authors and their precursors, highlighting the important links between language, creativity, and the coherent, organic presentation of a West Indian world view. We have shown that the precursors were merely precursors because, whereas their art contained some West Indian elements, it was not "West Indian" art. This contention was presented through an examination of elements of the structure and content of their works. It follows from what has been said about language that its use will provide us with the most important guide to "West Indianness" in Central American literature.

The Precursors: Language and Authenticity, the Glossary and Bilingualism

The precursors have indeed given ample evidence of the intent to attain authenticity in their portrayal of West Indian life and culture through a demonstration of familiarity with West Indian speech. They have seen quite clearly that the surest way to make their characters "real" is to make them speak like "real" West Indians. Of course, the ultimate level of authenticity is achieved when not only the characters but the authors themselves speak like West Indians. For, even granting the basic line of demarcation between character and author, this line can be and, in fact, is crossed in so far as the author creates a character who can speak—as the master poet, Nicolás Guillén, might have put it—"en antillano de verdad" (like an authentic West Indian).

Mélida Ruth Sepúlveda asserts that "the transcription of this language [i.e. West Indian Spanish] is one of the authentic positive aspects of his [i.e. Joaquín Beleño's] work."[2] However, Beleño's feelings about West Indians' language reflect his feelings about the people themselves: they cover the entire spectrum from exasperated disdain to enthusiastic acclaim. *Curundú* contains the author's most successful experiment in creating artistically realistic *"chombo"* talk. The very terms in which the following scene is presented make clear that, for all his profound familiarity with West Indian speech, it is something other than his. The scene consists of a conversation between Liequí and Tamtam in the presence of Rubén Galván (Beleño's alter ego). The conversation is introduced by Rubén's comments assessing the phenomenon of *"chombo"* speech, seen as: "A new language, up to a certain point, a mixture and alloy of English and Castilian. A jargon in which at times Spanish is used and at other times, English. And still others when it's neither one nor the other."[3] Rubén has some difficulty in fully following the conversation. It begins with Tamtam's intervention:

–Tú ve Liequí, el vacilón es así, spar (1) ...El vacilón! (2) Si tú te pones tof (3), tú te encuentras tu mamá y tu papá en la calle. Y esa boai! Tu sae bien a nosotro no guta vacilá aquí ... y ram, ahuecamo pa onde otro pedazo de gallina (4) que le guste el vacilón. Tú ve el vacilón ... ? (pp 135-136).

It is a macho conversation between two young "maleantes" (toughies), and this is certainly a factor affecting its representativeness as a sample of *"chombo"* speech. One notes immediately that Rubén's characterization of this language is substantially accurate. It is indeed a *jerga* (jargon), or, as the narrator describes it in similar circumstances in *Luna verde*, a "*caló.*"[5] However, it contains all of the features that the varieties of "*chombo*" speech employed in Beleño's work exhibit.

The most basic feature to which, for our purposes, all the others can be reduced is the need for a glossary of terms. In the short passage cited above there were four terms that had to be explained by the author's footnote. Two were obviously Spanish: *vacilón*, and *pedazo de gallina*, slang expressions. Two were taken directly from English: "spar," and "tof." "Spar" is the most interesting of these terms, since it comes directly from Jamaican Creole, and is consequently not fully understood by Beleño. He explains it as: "from the English, spark; a friend, companion; someone who sparks life in people" (p. 135). This is an explanation that amounts to an exercise in imaginative etymology.[6] Another interesting item is "boai," which is not footnoted here, since it was introduced elsewhere. It, of course, represents the phonetic spelling of "boy."[7] Beleño's characters use it to stand for simply "youth," masculine or feminine.[8] The ensuing four pages of this conversation are laced with words that the author has to explain: for example, "japi," "taim," "bier," "pritti," "uerquear," and "I si;" all of which are manifestly phonetic spellings of English words. The glossary of terms appears in all of Beleño's works, and, indeed, in all of the "West Indian" works by both the precursors and the West Indian authors themselves. Its size and accuracy will also be reliable indicators of the author's familiarity with "*chombo*" speech.

Whereas these four pages represent Beleño's most ambitious experiment with West Indian language, there are other samples in his trilogy. In *Luna verde*, for example, there is an instance in which the protagonist speaks of: "A *criollo* seated on a box, [who] complains because there could be no dancing in that room. He then goes on to recount some incident in his brand of *caló* ... ." With this introduction, the unnamed *criollo* begins a most interesting linguistic performance: "—Uasia boai! Ta mañana llega un buchí al 'machinchap' a buscá su cualquier yap y habla conmigo. Ai don min dat! Yo digo ..." (p. 50). The story he goes on to tell is about the "buchí" (man from the bush) who can only speak one word of English: "yes," and with this hopelessly inadequate preparation· foolhardily attempts to navigate the turbulent seas of the Canal Zone work place. The results are predictable, but this kind of story has very significant ramifications in Beleño's universe. When the "buchí" runs afoul of the brutally insensitive *gringo* foreman, he becomes the laughing stock of his fellow workers. He goes to the *criollo* for an explanation. From this source he learns that not only had the *gringo* fired him for not being able to speak English after apparently asserting that he could with his "yes" in response to the North American's "yu espikinglish," but the latter had in fact as well heaped abuse upon him, to which the poor "buchí's" only reply was a hollow "yes." His response to this explanation is to turn upon the West Indian, exhibiting the only too typical behavior of the oppressed, who wreak vengeance not on the oppressor but on the much more accessible fellow oppressed one.

It is his special use of language that makes for the intense symbolism of the pivotal scene discussed in Chapter One. Beleño is a convincing portrayer of West Indians because he understands their language, having had contact with them from his childhood. This is what the scene clearly affirms. Thus the imaginative etymologies and the creative orthography serve to heighten this impression by demonstrating that the author's knowledge comes not from books but from direct contact. Even in that very pivotal scene from *Curundú*, his English betrays him at times. When he has a West Indian exclaim: "Oh my God! ... — Cristí is died! Cristí is died!" (p. 120), or when he creates the following exchange between two supposed Afro-Antilleans:

> — Gerald? ... Oh, so sweet ...
> — Pearl ... Baby ... How are you ...? (p. 125)

the language is artificial. It appears to be a reconstruction that does not work. The second example fails for being too close to the so-called standard, not peculiarly West Indian. The first sample seems to be an attempt to incorporate some of the rules of "creole" grammar, but the resulting expression is not correct, neither in the creole usually spoken by Central American West Indians nor in any of the varieties of international standard English. These shortcomings are more than compensated for by the magic he weaves through the intensely sensitive display of his closeness to the *chombo* world. The simple term "Múfander," explained in his footnote as "from the English: Move from there" (p. 123), establishes beyond doubt this sensitivity. No expression could better convey a small *latino* boy's impression of a West Indian woman than this typical utterance of grown-ups to children. The very use of names: Miss Mery (not "Mary"), Mister Roach, for example, helps to magically capture the reality of West Indian life. The author himself uses in the language of narration at least one markedly creole form. For example: "Mister Roach's basin is full and the water on the floor is almost red, like *ceryl*" (p. 130, emphasis added). *Ceryl* represents the phonetic spelling of the Jamaican Creole version of "sorrel," and it is the spelling that is generally used by Beleño—for example in the glossary of *Luna verde*—probably supported by the practice of West Indian Panamanians.

Beleño makes much of the bilingualism that he considers, in general, to be an inescapable consequence of the dynamics of Panamanian history. He is somewhat resentful of this, as the implication in the opening sentence of his foreword to *Luna verde* strongly conveys: "The events we are about to witness are frequently defined with expressions of a strictly Saxon origin. We have deliberately decided to publish Ramón de Roquebert's diary with these deficiencies which detract from the integrity of the Spanish language ..." (n. pag.). The pronounced sense of humiliation and outrage at the imperialist presence is countered by a realization of the inevitability of colonialism, and by a basic respect for and attraction to the "superior" civilization. West Indian speech has the hatefulness of its association without the "redeeming" values imposed by economic power. However, Beleño yields to its persuasive charm and to its pervasive presence. Speaking through Ramón, he articulates this sentiment: "On the other hand, I consider myself obliged to accept the West Indianness of this city. ... The Creole aristocracy lives an insipid combination of Colombianism and Yankeeism, while the ordinary people live a brand of West Indianness implanted by this black sediment from the Caribbean islands" (pp. 178-9). The author declares that he will respect this reality. Thus bilingualism is an essential feature of a novel that depicts the life of West Indians, representing a recognition of the importance of West Indian speech. It overflows into the language of narration, as we have seen, thereby becoming more than just a device for creating authentic-sounding characters. It makes for an authentic-sounding novel.

Once again, then, Beleño has furnished a norm for assessing the art of the other precursors. In fact, his use of West Indian speech also gives us a yardstick for analyzing the creativity of the West Indian writers themselves. Through the need for authenticity in characterization he arrived at the necessity for bilingualism. This has given rise, as a consequence, to the use of the glossary of terms, a feature common to all regionalist-type literature, and one that has characterized those Spanish American works that were self-consciously "American."[9] The glossary gives the researcher or reader the distinct advantage of a quick and easy recourse for judging the breadth and depth of the author's familiarity with West Indian speech. Furthermore, it was shown that the bilingualism spills over into the author's language, as author. At this stage the author has almost created a West Indian work. However, because Beleño's frame of reference is always basically other than West Indian, for all his manifest empathy, he is essentially just a precursor. With the dawning of a Central American West Indian literature, the language as well as all other aspects of form and content would organically interrelate to the basic West Indian vision that essentially characterizes the work, and through which all other visions are presented.

Demetrio Aguilera Malta is an Ecuadorian, who, for all his chronological priority in the use of the West Indian theme in fiction, is totally unfamiliar with the language of Central American West Indians.[10] The Costa Rican Carlos Luis Fallas, whose *Mamita Yunai* preceded Beleño's work by a decade, at least recognized the importance of using West Indian speech in any attempt to depict, even partially, West Indian life and culture through characterization. However, Fallas, as he honestly admits in the autobiographical *Mamita Yunai*, did not understand English, neither the standard version nor the Jamaican Creole variety spoken by his black fellow citizens. This is made quite clear in the opening scene of the work, when the author/first-person narrator engages in conversation with one of the Afro-Antillean fellow travelers on the train: "I thought I recognized one of them, and, since he half-way spoke Spanish, I engaged him in conversation."[11] The recognition, quite doubtful, of the man is not the important factor, for, in those circumstances of enforced closeness through the confinement on the train, and the temporary but real camaraderie that obviously results, recognition would not be a necessary condition for communication. However, a common language is such a condition, and the common language here is the Spanish that the West Indian barely spoke. But Fallas's ignorance is not complete, the contact on the plantation with West Indians familiarized him with some basic lexical items. Like Beleño, he misunderstands the etymology and phonology of some of these items: for example, he explains "*sontín*" as "(from the English 'some time').—Food" (p. 221). He obviously fully understands the meaning of the lexical item, it is his linguistics that is faulty—as is only to be expected.[12] His linguistic weaknesses, unlike Beleño's, are not compensated for by any overwhelming display of sensitivity and exposure to any Central American Creole English.

In *Puerto Limón*, Joaquín Gutiérrez uses the blatant bilingualism and the grossly ungrammatical Spanish that were features of the speech of first- and second-generation West Indians.[13] He thereby gives an aura of authenticity to his Afro-Caribbean characters, Tom and Azucena. However, as we indicated earlier, these characters are very minor. Thus the use of West Indian language is quite restricted, there is not any need for a glossary. Fabián Dobles, and José León Sánchez, in like fashion, have used some degree of West Indian speech in the utterances they give to their Afro-Caribbean characters. But since the West Indianness is not a significant element in the works of either author, the use of such speech is consequently of relatively little consequence.

The West Indians: A New Spanish

"Mascon" Elements

In the literature that can be considered West Indian, the very language of the author has to be West Indian. The language of the characters in the precursors' works, and, to some extent, the language of the author—*per accidens*—in Beleño, has now to become identifiably the language of the work—*per se*. It is a point of fact that by the third and succeeding generations, the Afro-Caribbean people of Central America had become native speakers of Spanish, the official language. The language of the literature we have called West Indian is, then, essentially Spanish. What has to be seen now is how Quince Duncan, Gerardo Maloney, Cubena, and others using Spanish have created a literature that is West Indian sui generis. It is a language that has evolved through the dynamics of the struggle of an ethnolinguistic minority group for acceptance within the host community. Whether or not the solution followed the lines of the Flexibility-Synthesis or the Conflict-Replacement models is a question that is of pivotal importance, but one that must be shelved in a study such as this. The immediate concern must be exclusively with the end product of the process, examining its relevance to the creativity of the new West Indian authors from Central America; for these are the terms of the present research mandate.

The fact that the language of West Indians results as the end product of a torturous conflict with psychological as well as socioeconomic and political dimensions (referred to in the Introduction) underscores the poignancy of the very language itself. The choice of language by a member of the ethnolinguistic minority group bespeaks an attitude. It evokes a series of resonances deep within his soul, and these resonances, as indeed the attitude, have much to do with creativity and art. For all members of the group are poignantly conscious of the most important details of the collective conflict and relate instinctively and profoundly to any factor that draws particular reference to it, or to its most significant elements. It is difficult for an outsider to appreciate all of the complexities of this reality. However, the analysis must be attempted, especially because the situation of West Indians in Central America can be viewed as part of the larger reality of Caribbean cultural identity.

Since the new West Indian writers built on the contributions of the Beleños and the Gutiérrezes, etc, my analysis will follow the same lines as those developed in the study of the precursors, but will go beyond the question of glossaries and bilingualism to include the idea of identity and self-concept or definition. This development, of necessity, effects radical changes in the analysis. To account fully for the heightened intensity of the significance of language, I have opted to include a line of approach developed by Professor Stephen Henderson in his extremely insightful work, *Understanding the New Black Poetry*.[14] Professor Henderson introduced the concept of "mascon" words and constructions. They are: "Certain words and constructions [which] seem to carry an inordinate charge of emotional and psychological weight, so that whenever they are used they set all kinds of bells ringing, all kinds of synapses snapping, on all kinds of levels" (p. 44). He further explains that these are more than mere so-called "code words," and more too than those words deemed by conventionally literary criticism to have "resonance." He specifies: "I am speaking rather of words which are innocent enough—words like 'rock,' 'roll,' 'jelly,' 'bubber,' 'jook,' and the like, which have levels of meaning that seem to go back to our earliest grappling with the English language in a strange and hostile land. These words, of course, are used in complex associations, and thus form meaningful wholes in ways which defy understanding by outsiders" (p. 44). The term "mascon" is, as Henderson explains, a borrowing from NASA's (The National Aeronautics and Space Administration) invented acronym to refer to "massive concentrations" of matter. The "mascon" terms and constructions evoke "a massive concentration of Black experiential energy which powerfully affects the meaning of Black speech, Black song, and Black poetry ..." (p. 44). "Mascon" linguistic elements must exist in all cultures,[15] but it is reasonable to assert that they are likely to occur more frequently and to be more powerfully significant among a people that has a fresh experience with intense struggle against a common set of problems. Such are the ethnolinguistic minority groups of Panama and Costa Rica.[16] "Mascon" terms evidently do not need to be defined for the in-group, however, a glossary is necessary for the general reader.

It would seem clear that the most obvious "mascon" terms would be those that evoke with naked directness the primordial sense of belonging to the ethnolinguistic minority group. Such would be the special names by which the group is identified, conjuring up the specter of the differential factor that marks it off from the rest of the society. The designations, "chumeca," "chumecaman," "jamaiquino," "jamaicano," and "chombo" (see note 7 of the Introduction), used to refer to Central American West Indians are the ones that have historically generated the most massive concentrations of negative energy. They have been used in varying degrees as racial slurs. In fact, the term "chombo" in Panama corresponds roughly to "nigger" in the United States. It is precisely with this term, "chombo," that Cubena has achieved a reversal of the negative energy. Taking possession of the insult he has hurled it back into the faces of his would-be vilifiers as a defiant cry of self-assertion. In exactly the same manner, "nigger" has been used by some Afro-Americans and nègre was used by the launchers of the Negritude movement in Paris of the 1930's.[17] Cubena's first novel is entitled simply, Chombo.[18] It is a work that proudly proclaims on almost every page the selfhood of West Indian Panamanians, establishing resoundingly the "mascon" nature of the term. (Chapter Four presents a full analysis of this novel).

The names of persons do indeed pertain to this special class of words and expressions, for it is by their individual names that Central American West Indians have been marked apart from the mainstream population group. The names of Duncan's main characters are, for example, the primary indicators of West Indianness. Charles McForbes and his first true love, Lorena Sam, as well as Cristian Bowman, Ruth Viales, Clarita Drake, Alfred George, and others from Los cuatro espejos are all cases in point. The touching story of conjugal love that gives the title to his first collection of short stories, Una canción en la madrugada, has as its protagonists Juan and Mayra. Sitaira Kenton, Pedro Dull and Cato Brown are the main characters in the pivotal plot of La paz del pueblo, and Jose Gordon is the protagonist of "La leyenda de Jose Gordon," from La rebelion pocomia y otros relatos.

Cubena, too, peoples his fictional universe with characters who are identifiably West Indian by their very names. He dedicates his Cuentos del negro Cubena to Papa James and Nenen, who appear in "Luna de miel" as James Douglin and Lena McZeno.[20] His novel Chombo ambitiously seeks to make the entire group of West Indian Panamanians its protagonist. In this work the mere mention of names is sufficient to evoke the massive concentrations of experiential energy, and these kinds of evocations, that occur quite frequently, constitute the core of Cubena's narrative. We are told, for instance: "Among the workers to arrive on this trip were the brothers David, Silvester, and Samuel Williams, who hailed from the village of Xaymaca-Nokoró" (p. 38). Or, later in the novel, the simple fact is stated to the effect that Nenen had to establish a little business enterprise "in order to better afford the token fees charged by Teacher Phillips and the other West Indian teachers, like Céspedes Burke, Sidney Grant, Russell Phillips, Barton" (p. 49). The first passage illustrates, in addition to the use of the "mascon" potential of Anglophone West Indian names, how Cubena has creatively developed even further this process. Xaymaca-Nokoró represents a harking back to the authentic indigenous Caribbean as well as the African roots. Of course, the process is based on Cubena's erudition, but the sentiments it seeks to evoke are special to all Caribbean people. (See Chapter Four for more on this matter).

The poets— Maloney, for example—also realize that the resonances stirred in the hearts and minds of their fellow Central American West Indians by the mere mention of certain names are still vibrant and poetically viable. He conjures up this magic by pronouncing such names in a poetic incantation in his "Testimonios" (Testimonies). To the outsider this incantation may appear to be no more than an enumeration:

> Rupert — With his own hands he planted dozens of buildings in Balboa
> Jahn — Now in his father's retirement, he watches the door and the tourists' steps
>
> . . . .
>
> Ginger — Dreamt about becoming a paratrooper[21]

In response to his summons the poet has each one of those named manifest some key to his or her innermost secret self. All the keys are identifiable markers of—testimonies to—the West Indian experience in Panama.

Abel Pacheco too shows some willingness to use the technique, and titles one of his prose poems of the collection, *Más abajo de la piel*, "Papá Uriah." The name with its heavy biblical resonances is charged with the spirit of the British West Indies, where the imposing names of the Old Testament, Uriah, Hezekiah, Jubal, Ebenizer, are borne with simple nobility by so many common people. The poem is indeed an evocation of the old days of the West Indian presence in Costa Rica, based on the "testimony" of Papa Uriah as the introductory line, "An old old man told me ...," proclaims.[22]

Beleño and the precursors evidently understood the sociological relevance of the West Indians' names. Their characters bear distinctive names that label them in one way or another. Beleño, for example, has created: Tamtam (Tom-tom), Red Box (a "red nigger" or "high yellow," in Beleño's language a "*chombo blanco*"), and, of course, Atá. This latter form represents Beleño's rendition of the creole pronunciation of Arthur. (What Beleño must have heard was Atá—with two accented "a's," he seems to have paid attention only to the final accent). Fallas's chief Afro-Caribbean character is "mister Clinton" from *Mamita Yunai*, and Fabián Dobles has his Sammy, from *El jaspe*.[23]

All the writers have captured a detail of usage that for all its apparent insignificance does really contribute to the distinctiveness of West Indian culture and life. It is the use of the title to prefix the proper and not the surname: for example, Miss Mary, and Mr. Charles—or in the terms used by all the authors, "mister" (fully spelled out). This form of address is certainly neither

44

native nor peculiar to the Anglophone Caribbean. However, its use is quite common among the people of this region as a medium for manifesting the profoundly African sense of respect for elders and ancestors. The form may even be heard between wife and husband, and certainly within the West Indian tradition it would be unthinkable for a child or youth to address a grown-up by his or her first name without some prefix to denote respect. When "Uncle" or "Aunt" (and its more frequently used variants "Auntie" or "Tantie") would not be appropriate, "Miss" or "Mister" would be obligatory. All of this is captured in such a simple expression as, for example, "Miss Mary."

Nenen of Cubena's universe has been named with a term that must be considered to belong to the "mascon" group. F. G. Cassidy and R. B. Le Page define it as: "sb dial. var. of NANA c.f. Twi 'nàña' grandmother, and Efik 'n' né,' term of address to an old woman."[24] This title of address that comes directly from Africa has been fashioned into a proper name: the name of a pivotal West Indian figure in both Cubena's fictional and nonfictional worlds. Nenen's companion in life in Cubena's fictional unviverse is Papa James. The usage that this latter expression bespeaks is one that has become significant in Caribbean cultures by virtue of its frequency. "Papa Uriah" (referred to earlier) is, of course, another example of this usage. Cubena also uses the term "graní," a Hispanicization of "grannie," with full "mascon" effect in Chombo—it is used interchangeably with "nenen."

The Anancy or Nancy stories recounting the exploits of cunning Brother Spider (Anancy) are not restricted to the Jamaican Ashantis. They enliven the culture of West Indian people in other islands, Trinidad for example. Duncan has introduced Anancy into his narrative universe as Hermano Araña, using this figure as a symbol and indicator of the West Indian presence. This kind of use is singularly appropriate in a novel such as La paz del pueblo, a poetic work rich in symbolism that is always complex even to the point of obscurity at times. Hermano Araña and other perhaps not so well-known figures of folk mythology like Bukú and Balí evoke strong feelings of identity in the reader. In the following passage: "There are memories that flow in the blood, old legends, fables that the wind whispers at night, and Sister shaken by the cry that suddenly filled the village, the cry of an animal of prey, and Brother Spider..." (p. 101) the mythical aura of the folktale is incorporated into the narrative and adds to the magical effect of the work. In this precise context, in the very same long sentence—it constitutes the entire paragraph—we read: "... because the cursed traitors Bukú and Balí had invaded the sacred village violating the domains of the Samamfo..." (p. 101.)—"Samamfo" will be explained in Chapter Three. In one stroke the author has employed three names whose "mascon" potential is evident.

Hermano Tucumá is another similar folklore figure whose mention is used in the novel to evoke strong feelings of cultural identity. Speaking of Cornelio, Sitaira's (the main female protagonist) once macho father, who has been rendered paralyzed and impotent by an accident, the author creates the following paragraph: "One single tale hammered at his memory, a tale about

Hermano Araña and *Hermano Tucumá* that someone, a woman, had told him a half hour before the accident" (p. 68). The hammering metaphor is equal to the huge impact of the "mascon" folk symbol.

Every society develops some peculiar expressions and exclamations that have no meaning outside of the group. In some cases these may be lexical items common to the language, in other cases they are not. One such expression is "cho." It is defined by Cassidy and Le Page as "An exclamation expressing scorn, impatience, annoyance, disagreement, expostulation, etc. usually independent; also preceding a statement or question." Two etymons are cited for this Jamaican Creole expression: the "Ewe tsóò, an interjection of anger, impatience, disappointment, and the Twi, *twéaa*, an interjection of uttermost contempt." its use in the following situation created by Duncan illustrates the artistic value of this "mascon" lexical item. It appears in the idyllic but real love story, "Una canción en la madrugada," the initial work of a collection having the same title, Duncan's first published compilation of short stories. The protagonists Juan and Mayra are a married, working-class West Indian couple from Limon. They have children and many responsibilities. Yet they manage one Sunday to slip away by themselves on a picnic by the river. With gleeful anticipation, and perhaps with the thrill of recollection of their days of courtship, they prepare to take a swim in the river:

—You're brave enough to bathe here?
—There aren't any crocodiles?
—Well I guess way out there yes.
—Where do you want us to bathe then?
—Here ... right here in the stream ... it's deep enough.
—And they don't come round by here?
—No man, cho! (p. 17)

This conversational interlude captures the spirit of a typical exchange between husband and wife, and ends with the "cho," the most eloquent expression of this spirit. The Jamaican Creole expression is tastefully woven into the fabric of a passage in conversational Spanish without any trace of stereotypic and gross bilingualism. There is nothing ungrammatical in this language that is so true-to-life, so Costa Rican yet renedered resoundingly West Indian by the final "cho." The Afro-Caribbean reader will immediately react with a feeling of identification, the comfort of recognizing that "now, they're talking my language." Throughout his works, Duncan employs "cho" in a manner consistent with the use in the above passage.

The very Jamaican forms "raas" and "raatid" have not been used by Duncan nor by any of the West Indian writers in any similarly artistic fashion. Pacheco in *Más abajo de la piel* uses the form "turrass" (p. 63), and Beleño in *Curundú* has Cristí (the same Cristí presented in Chapter One) say: "Too much cold—turass" (p. 118). Since "raas" is a vulgar expression evolved probably—according to Cassidy and Le Page—from a metathesis of "arse," it is not surprising that its "mascon" potential has gone so far untapped by the West Indian authors.

It may be convincingly argued that under certain socioeconomic conditions created by a particular historical process, food items can become a source of intense cultural identification providing a rallying point around which the members of a group can marshall their experiential energies. In the Central American situation West Indians and *latinos* (of the white/mestizo, or *"paña"* variety) sometimes square off culturally over the question of the relative value of their distinctive patterns of nutrition and the items that constitute these patterns. Thus in *Mamita Yunai*, Fallas speaks dismissively of "an infusion of leaves that the black folks call tea and that only they can stomach" (p. 176). The reference is most probably to *"sorocí"* tea, the Hispanicized version of "cerosee" and "cerasee," which Cassidy and Le Page explain is "valued in Jamaica as a 'tea-bush' to clear the blood." The lexical item *"sorocí"* is defined by Duncan in *La paz del pueblo* as a *"planta medicinal"* (a medicinal plant) (p. 193). It enjoys the same kind of esteem in the Afro-Caribbean communities as do the various health foods in contemporary United States culture.

Foods like akee and codfish for Jamaicans, and crab and callaloo for Trinidadians, or flying fish and cuckoo for Barbadians have distinct national significance. In parallel fashion Central American West Indians respond passionately (as well as gastronomically) to foods like bammy, yam, yampee, bake, souse, patty, escoveitched fish, and black pudding. They perceive that the use of these foods not only fortifies the body but refreshes the spirit by affirming cultural roots. Such affirmation is crucial for an ethnolinguistic minority group.

Cubena's Nenen, in real life as well as in fiction (in *Cuentos del negro Cubena*) established a roadside stall where she sold West Indian food: "Besides, every night, at the corner of 21st and 3rd of November, she sold *chicheme*, *bollos*, *carimañolas*, bakes, souse, pigeon pea soup, patties, fried fish, escoveithced fish, black pudding, *sancocho, guacho"* (p. 34). In the later work, *Chombo*, the list has evolved: "At the crowded street corner the clients savored coconut rice with pigeon peas, codfish, fried fish, souse, patties, bakes, fried casava, black pudding, *bofe*, potato salad, *patacones, carimañolas* .... And to drink there was *chicheme*, sorrel, gingerbeer and other beverages" (p. 105). The second listing is a more complete one. In both, the Anglophone versions, "bake," "souse," and the barely Hispanic *"patí,"* are used. In addition in the second list sorrel (in Cubena's version of the Hispanicized form, *saril*— somewhat different from Beleño's *ceryl*), and "gingerbeer" (un-Hispanicized) also appear. The author has learned to better use the "mascon" potential of the terms, for obviously their Anglophone versions evoke much more direct and intense sentiments of identity. It might be noted that what I have translated as "escoveitched fish" appears in Spanish as *"ceviche"*; however, I am convinced that what Cubena intended was most accurately rendered by this translation. Furthermore, not all of the food items mentioned in the two lists come from the islands—this is not surprising.

Duncan, in *Los cuatro espejos*, uses the food item *yuca con bofe* in a manner reminiscent of Ralph Ellison's transcendental use of yam in *Invisible Man*.[25] When, in the same novel, Duncan wishes to evoke the past days of the happy life Charles and Lorena shared, rooted in the West Indian community, he draws on the "mascon" power of food: "Stretched out in bed, defenseless, beaten, she would think about all that. And about her love too. Because it was love that made her get up morning after morning for so many years to fix his breakfast (bammy, breadfruit, roast plantain)" (p. 84). I am personally familiar with Central American West Indians resident in the United States who would be stimulated almost to the point of salivation upon reading the parenthesized portion of the above quotation. This is precisely the kind of effect intended by the author.[26]

Their religious experience being of such cultural importance, it has provided many "mascon" terms for West Indians. "Obeah" is perhaps the most important of such terms. Duncan provides a lengthy explanation in the glossary of *La paz del pueblo*:

> power. ... Afro-Caribbean cosmology presents (at least in its Limon version) a triangular vision of reality: in one of the angles of a triangle we could represent God, in the other the powers of the living dead and in the other the power of the living. Man, placed in the center of the triangle, is under the influence of the forces mentioned. (p. 192)

Cassidy and Le Page in their explanation add the idea that "in practice it has never been clearly distinguished from MYAL, though the latter was supposedly curative of the ills caused by the former." The term has currency in the popular language of practically every Caribbean community. (Its equivalent in popular U.S. culture would be "voodoo"). The Mighty Sparrow, the Trinidadian calypsonian, has sung at least two eminently successful calypsoes on the theme of obeah: "Melda" and "Witch Doctor." Claude McKay, in his pivotal West Indian novel, *Banana Bottom* (1933), makes significant use of the question of obeah. It recurs with regularity in West Indian fiction, for example, in Alfred Mendes' *Black Fauns* (1934), in V. S. Naipaul's *The Mystic Masseur* (1957), in Ismith Khan's *The Obeah Man* (1964), and in Orlando Patterson's *The Children of Sisyphus* (1971).[27]

In *Los cuatro espejos* Lorena Sam, the key female protagonist, as well as Ruth, her intimate friend, and Christian Bowman, her frustrated suitor, were all children of "*obeahmanes*," to use Duncan's version of the Hispanicized plural of the term "obeah men." So important a word has to be fully incorporated into the Spanish language of West Indian Central Americans, and the existence of the plural from "*obeahmanes*" is eloquent testimony to this incorporation. Cubena, in fact, has developed the process even further, creating the form "*obeá*."

Duppies populate the world of Jamaican folk belief. Duncan's definition, in *La paz del pueblo*, of these entities is quite similar to that of Cassidy and Le Page, albeit much briefer: "apparition, spirit of a dead person" (p. 191). The central action of *Los cuatro espejos*, the death of Lorena and the final breakdown of Charles's harmonious interaction with, and sense of belonging to, his West Indian community, comes about as a direct result of the malignant intervention of a *"dopí."* Señora Mariot, from *La paz del pueblo*, in a poetically introspective passage that is woven from the fabric of Pedro's (the main male character) perceptions refers to: "My specters, the duppies [*dopíes* in the original Spanish] that come into my room at night, to watch with me while I passionately weep over my lack of tears, and life goes by in iniquitous silence ..." (p. 168). *Dopí* and *dopíes*, then, like *obeá, obeah, obeahman*, and *obeahmanes*, have passed into the language and universe of Central America's West Indian writers.

Kumina and Pukumina are household terms to most Jamaicans and indeed to many other Caribbean people. Leonard Barrett, an expert on Caribbean and other Afro-American cultures, gives the etymology of Kumina as follows: "The word comes from two Twi words: *Akom*—'to be possessed,' and *Ana*—'by an ancestor.'"[28] He claims that this is a case, one of many, of the carry-over of the Twi language of the Ashanti people into the everyday speech of present-day Jamaicans. Kumina is then for him a folk religion of the African people who have become natives of Jamaica. It is related to Myal, the benign counterpoint to obeah (and as Cassidy and Le Page point out, the distinction between the two is frequently blurred in the popular mind). Kumina was originally the "rigorous dance" which accompanied the Myal—"being in a state of possession"— ritual.[29] Finally, Kumina can refer to the actual service itself in which the dance of possession is the central act. Pukumina is described by Barrett as an Afro-Christian syncretic sect which, of the three most important in Jamaica, is the most African in its rituals and beliefs. Cassidy and Le Page explain that the obviously related form "pocomania," was established by a false Hispanicizing of a probably African form "pu + kumona." What emerges from all this is that the terms Kumina and Pukumina exhibit the phonological dynamism that frequently characterizes the most widely used lexical items, and that they are clear examples of Africanisms in Jamaican speech.

The same forms appear in Duncan's work as *"cuminá"* and *"pocomía"*— true Hispanicizations of the original Jamaican Creole words. He defines *"Cuminá"* in the glossary of *La pa. del pueblo* as simply, *"dios* [god]" (p. 191). The term *"pocomía"* is itself used in the very title of the author's latest collection of short stories, *La rebelión pocomía*. Such is also the title of the initial story of the collection; a story of a rebel figure, like Pedro (of *La paz del pueblo*), who is a special devotee of *"Cuminá."* Like Pedro, too, his source of strength comes from his participation in the "Hermandad Pocomía" (Pukumina Brotherhood). These two cases demonstrate Duncan's artistic use of terms that evoke massive concentrations of experiential energy among West Indian Costa Ricans. He has built the "mascon" nature of the terms into the very structure of two of his most important works by incorporating them into the plot and characterization—to be seen in the next chapter.

An Artistic Bilingualism

In Cubena's narrative the characters are often made to revert to the basic kind of bilingualism that was so characteristic of Beleño, Fallas, and the precursors in general. At times either their Spanish is interspersed with Jamaican Creole (Panamanian English) words and expressions, or they are made to speak entirely in a version of English. This is done in the interest of historical accuracy, for indeed the fictive persons made to speak in this manner are the early immigrants. For example, in *Chombo* Cubena has a Jamaican Creole dialogue between Nenen and her mother, the dialogue taking place on the boat during the crossing from Jamaica to Panama (p. 42). With equal historical verisimilitude he has his first- and second-generation West Indian Panamanian characters frequently cite Jamaican Creole proverbs and sayings. For example, Leonora Dehaney, a first-generation immigrant, utters: *"Cuss-cuss never bore hole in a man kind"* (p. 51). And later on in the same reported conversation she is made to say. *"paña machete cut two sides."* This utterance represents a special case of linguistic syncretism, for *"machete"* is a fully Spanish word that has been adopted into the creole speaker's lexicon and *"paña"* is a "Spanish" word invented by creole speakers: an aphetic form of *"España"* (Spain), it refers to those white/mestizo fellow countrymen whose language and racial background make them "real Spanish," in the perception of the West Indians.

In further pursuit of fidelity to historical circumstances, Cubena even attempts to create a mixture of French and English Creoles with Spanish, the kind of fascinating speech that he rightly imagines must have been used in the early days. Tidam Frenchí, a first generation migrant from the Francophone Caribbean, chides her daughter thus: *"—Luisa, pour cuá tú no cocinar like petit sistá Aldita?"* (p. 52). *"Pour cuá"* (from the French *"pourquoi"* —"why"— and split into two words in imitation of the corresponding Spanish form *"por qué"*) and *"petit"* (from the French *"petite"* — little —) represent Cubena's version of the French Creole input. *"Tú no cocinar"* (don't you cook) is a historically accurate rendition of the tentative Spanish spoken by the early immigrants, and even the second generation. The need for this kind of experimentation diminishes as the setting for the narrative approaches the contemporary period, and consequently the instances of its use are quite few.

Cubena takes the experimentation one step further and creates an artistic bilingualism based on Spanish and Twi (the language of the Ashanti ancestors). This kind of language is not meant to mirror any historically real speech patterns but to symbolize the vital significance of the African cultural heritage. The following excerpt taken from "La abuelita africana," from *Cuentos del negro Cubena*, illustrates the technique: "At twilight one evening, an *erubinrin* (female slave) gave birth to an *omobinrin* (daughter) in a canefield..." (p. 78). The story is structured on two chronological levels, one present the other past, which are skillfully interwoven. The narrative corresponding to the past is written in italics, in parentheses, and employs the Twi/Spanish bilingual technique through the artificial insertion of Twi words. The technique is used again in the highly symbolic final chapter of Chombo. The novel's seven chapters are also given titles in Twi, for example, "Ebenada" and "Wukuada," each one signifying a day of the week.

Cubena, Maloney, Duncan, Bernard, and obviously Pacheco write in Spanish. So too do the other West Indian poets from Central America whose work is even more incipient or who have received even less exposure than the four mentioned: for example, David McField and Carlos Rigby of Nicaragua; and the Panamanians, Luis Carlos Phillips, Urá del Drago, Walter Smith, Winston Churchill James, among others. Their artistic language is definitely incompatible with the cruder forms of bilingualism. In fact, even Cubena's glossary at the end of Chombo is significantly a glossary of "panameñismos" (Panamanianisms), not "chombismos" nor "antillanismos." In the terms of Ramirez, III's disjunction they have opted for the Flexibility-Synthesis model, for their Spanish can certainly be termed "West Indian" while retaining its essential Hispanicity. It is clear, especially in the case of Cubena, whose linguistic sensibilities are much more finely developed than those of the other West Indians, that this position is a conspicuously worked out artistic solution. Athough the process of choice is not a clearly documented in Duncan's, Maloney's, nor in Bernard's written work, the language that emerges in their cases is just as much an artistic "West Indian" Spanish. Their language, too, taps the aesthetic potential of the peculiar dynamic of the Central American West Indian ethnolinguistic minority group, eliciting powerful sentiments in their Afro-Caribbean readers.

Carlos E. Russell, a Panamanian West Indian who like Cubena now lives and works in the U.S., has written a book of poems in English—with one significant exception, "Quién soy?"[30] He is representative of those Central American West Indians, and there are many, who have opted for the Anglophone alternative. Whereas Bernard, a Costa Rican, has, on the other hand, maintained the highest level of flexibility and synthesis in her oral poetry (available on an LP record), which is totally bilingual in Spanish and English of both the creole and the "standard" varieties, her written work is understandably fully Hispanic.

It could be said by way of summary that literary works about the life and culture of Central American West Indians a priori have to build on the rich linguistic heritage.[31] The preceding discussion has shown that a posteriori they have done so. Through the judicious use of "mascon" words and expressions, and through an artistic bilingualism, West Indian writers from Central America have created a literary language that attests to the appropriateness of the designation I have chosen. In this area of their artistic enterprise, as in others, they have been guided by the example of the "precursors." However, they have again surpassed these latter, for their (i.e. the West Indians') language is harmoniously related to a world view that is essentially and coherently West Indian.

CHAPTER THREE

RELIGION IN THE NARRATIVE OF QUINCE DUNCAN*

Quince Duncan, born in 1940, is the "senior" of the West Indian writers under consideration, his literary output far surpassing that of the others. He has published two collections of short stories: *Una canción en la madrugada* (1970) and *La rebelión pocomía y otros relatos* (1976); four novels: *Hombres curtidos* (1971)—which is out of print and unavailable—*Los cuatro espejos* (1973), *La paz del pueblo* (1978), and *Final de calle* (1979).[1] In addition he has written two studies: *El negro en la literatura costarricense* (1975) and, in collaboration with Carlos Meléndez, *El negro en Costa Rica* (1972).[2] His work has not been adequately studied, even in his native Costa Rica. This chapter will focus on the religious theme in the Duncan fictional universe. The second part of the chapter will briefly examine the other areas of what can be considered the West Indian features of this universe.

West Indian Religious Elements

Anthropologists see religion as the cementing factor in all African cultures. John S. Mbiti, for example, opens his work *African Religions and Philosophy* with the bald assertion: "Africans are notoriously religious."[3] He goes on, on the same page, to say: "Religion is the strongest element in traditional background, and exerts probably the greatest influence upon the thinking and living of the people concerned [the African people]." Edward Brathwaite, one of the most outstanding poet-intellectuals in the contemporary Caribbean, restates Mbiti's insight significantly strengthened by the input of other scholars when he claims: "And everyone agrees that the focus of African culture in the Caribbean was religious."[4] Duncan was born and raised in the heavily Afro-Caribbean province of Limón, in the bosom of a community permeated with Afro-based religious sentiment. He has himself commented on this religiousness, concluding in concert with general anthropological opinion that not only is it central to the life

---

*A shorter version of this chapter has appeared as, "Religious Elements in the Narrative of Quince Duncan," *Afro-Hispanic Review*, 1, No. 2 (May 1982), 27-31.

and culture of West Indians from Limón but that it is marked by a spirit of tolerance for the other.[5]

Imbued with the particular religiousness of his native milieu, Duncan developed beyond the norm, for he became an Anglican priest. This implies a particularly complex personal religious experience, since Anglicanism as the prestige religion in the community certainly won for its ministers the highest degree of respect among a people especially sensitized to religion, and extraordinarily tolerant of variation. However, for all the respect and tolerance, and the syncretic tendency on the part of West Indians, they continued to live in a world in which their way of life was different from, considered inferior to, and, consequently, in essential conflict with that of the dominant group. In the community in general the fundamental internal dynamic of the syncretic process would be countered by the basic sense of conflict imposed by its necessary interaction with the mainstream. In Duncan these two governing modes, syncretism/tolerance and conflict, that shaped the religious perspective of his people would be especially important because his personal experience with religion was more intense even than that of his fellow Afro-Caribbean people in Limón.

These considerations provide an effective line of approach for our analysis of the religious theme, namely, the examination of the concepts of syncretism and conflict in Duncan's presentation of religion especially in relation to the characterization and basic plot in his fictional universe.

Syncretism

It is generally accepted that syncretism is one of the important features of New World African cultures. By very definition it is a pivotal factor in the development of the various New World creole languages.[6] Melville Herskovits is one of the first of contemporary anthropologists to report in a systematic fashion on syncretism in "neo-African" religions of the Americas. The evidence of religious syncretism is plain for all to see. I, for example, have witnessed Shango[7] ceremonies in my native Trinidad and Tobago in which there were obvious admixtures of Catholic liturgy and symbolism: the making of the sign of the cross, the use of an altar closely resembling that in a Catholic church with figures of Catholic saints (all white) along with flowers and candles. Analogous syncretic features, that is, the blending of West African religious elements with various Euro-Christian ones (either Catholic or Protestant) are patently present in the Santería, the Candomblé, and the Voodoo religions of Cuba, Brazil, and Haiti respectively; as well as in the Kumina and Pukumina religions of Jamaica (already discussed in Chapter Two), or in the so-called "small churches" of the Caribbean.[8]

Rooted in the profound adaptability or tolerance of the traditional African spirit, syncretism was an important survival mechanism for African religiosity during the oppressive days of colonization and slavery. By adopting the mere outward trappings of the prevailing Christian relgion, the New World Africans could continue to practice their age-old religions under the very noses of the oppressors. Eminently suited as it was to the barbaric conditions of underdevelopment imposed by Europeans, it does not owe its development exclusively to these conditions. Herskovits, in fact, reports on a case of syncretism in Africa, during the epoch prior to Europe's brutal incursion, "between Mohammedan *jinn* and Hausa *'iska.*"[9] Along analogous lines, Leonard Barrett claims (see Chapter Two) that Kumina represents as well a syncretism of various distinctive patterns of African ethnic rituals under the one Ashanti rubric. This kind of all-African syncretism is a feature also of Shango, *Santería, Candomblé,* and Voodoo. In the first three Yoruba as well as non-Yoruba elements are included under a Yoruba rubric, in the last it is the Dahomean rubric that provides the cover encompassing other non-Dahomean elements.[10]

Duncan's treatment of the theme of obeah in *Los cuatro espejos* demonstrates the important artistic impact that syncretism can be made to have on plot and characterization.[11]. The novel tells the story of a young West Indian, Charles McForbes, who, although educated into the religion and culture of the white world, returns to his native village as a part-time Anglican pastor and a full-time peasant. His life is destroyed when his wife, Lorena, also a West Indian from Limón, is attacked by a duppy in broad daylight, and sustains a mysterious illness which neither the force of obeah nor the light of modern science and medicine can cure. She dies after a prolonged stay in the hospital in the nation's capital, and Charles eventually abandons his village life, taking up residence definitively in the capital, and marrying into one of the principal families of the white/mestizo dominant group. The novel begins with Charles's psychological trauma brought on by what turns out to be a crisis of identity. Frantically seeking a cure for the trauma he finally makes a physical return to his native village, and this appears to resolve his conflict somewhat.

Charles's most fundamental character trait is his syncretism: he is a man of at least two worlds. His double identity is most glaringly manifested through his religion, for he is an Anglican pastor, an upholder of the principles of the prestige European religion, but he is completely at home with his West Indian folk steeped in their Afro-oriented culture. His life is intimately caught up in syncretism, and indeed conflict. For example, shortly after what must have been his first return to Limón fresh from his secondary and post-secondary studies in a seminary in the capital, the new part-time pastor is confronted with a problem of low productivity on his land. The narrator presents the matter as an obvious case of the interference of praeternatural forces, and his character Charles, as a matter of course, has recourse to an obeah man. The latter's prescriptions do indeed prove to be the exact remedy for the situation, for time proves that Charles's original suspicions and interpretation of the problem were correct: the low productivity was the result of the activity of another obeah man engaged by his rival, Cristian Bowman. What is more impressive is the fact that Charles's wife, the object of Cristian's long-standing sexual desires, is herself the offspring of a highly reputed obeah man. In fact, it is to his father-in-law that the beleagured pastor turns with such success.

The success is only temporary, for one day while Charles is working on the land he is called home dramatically to learn that his wife has been attacked by a *dopí*, with the fatal consequences already mentioned. It is suggested that this nefarious duppy was commissioned by Cristian, but there is no certainty of this in the enigmatically structured novel with its inverted and fragmented chronology, its symbolism, and its basic vagueness—frequently encountered features of the modern novel. What is certain is that Charles McForbes at this period of his life is fully integrated into the West Indian community, and obeah is the medium through which this integration is most effectively manifested to the reader.

Pedro Dull, the main character of *La paz del pueblo*, is to Kumina what Charles is to obeah.[12] Kumina represents for Duncan not only a syncretism of various African rituals and beliefs but more importantly it exists as one integral element of a total milieu in which Christian beliefs and practice constitute another fundamental element. Pedro's basic function in the novel springs from his syncretic nature. Like Charles, he is the product of a merging of two worlds and this circumstance accounts for both his nature and his role in the novel: a role that is harmoniously integrated into the central element of the plot.

Pedro is something of an enigma; a lonely and basically troubled character of deliberately obscured origin, he has much in common with the existentialist hero. The mystery and uncertainty that enshroud him and indeed the entire work are a function of the extremely convoluted structure that may remind the reader of another famous Latin American novel about another Pedro, *Pedro Páramo* (1955), by the Mexican Juan Rulfo.[13] Pedro's centrality in *La paz del pueblo* only takes definite shape in the final sections. This final movement towards centrality begins especially with a series of insinuations thrown significantly from the pulpit by an unnamed pastor. This voice berates those people, "persons who are not even from here," outsiders who have come to disturb "the peace of this village" (p. 149). The terms are, of course, eminently significant since they enter into the title of the entire work itself, *La paz del pueblo* (The peace of the people / village). It turns out that the disturbers of the peace referred to are followers of Marcus Garvey, who, in the benighted view of the unnamed pastor is not a liberator of his people but one who would return them to the "barbarism" of "pagan" Africa. The Garveyites and proponents of the general banana workers strike are inveighed against by the preacher principally because they jeopardize the interests of a prominent church member. Pedro, then, is the symbol of this outside presence committed to the banana strike as the sole means of restoring dignity to the people; he is above all a follower of Marcus Garvey.

The pace of the final movement picks up, when the author reveals the true source of the strength with which Pedro resists oppression. Employing the technique of flashback, the key to the understanding of the work is presented in the most direct fashion. Pedro is a practitioner of the Pukumina religion (*pocomía*). He has been initiated into it by the same Mama Bull who appears in the title story of the collection *La rebelión pocomía y otros relatos*.[14] His very participation in the ritual represents an important step on the road to revolution, for he does it against the wishes of his mother, impelled by his vocation to service and conquering his own initial resistance to the call of Cuminá. The text states explicitly: "And the young man tried to obey his mother, but time and time again *Cuminá* came back with his secret messages" (p. 174). *Cuminá* takes possession of him in the course of the ritual during a dance, and Pedro dances the dance of *Cuminá*. Under *Cuminá's* influence his revolutionary consciousness develops; he sees the glories of the African past; he sees the need for justice in the neocolonial present. He renounces the false laws of the oppressor in this fundamental declaration to his mother: "The fact is that we did not make the law! Our law remained in Africa!" (p. 174). Having attained this stage of consciousness, he is ready to receive the doctrines of Garvey. Now that he is a complete rebel, his mother gives up definitively on him, and, as the text states with bald simplicity, "from that moment he began to die" (p. 175). The author reiterates that Pedro through his dancing under possession by *Cuminá* becomes a rebel: becomes a man. The idea that rebellion is the only possible posture for the real man in the colonized context is one that has been espoused by many Caribbean artists and intellectuals, Aimé Césaire and Frantz Fanon being the most prominent. Pedro's rebellion is no different from that of the rebel character at the heart of Césaire's plays, and his point of view is consistent with that prescribed by Fanon in his pivotal, *The Wretched of the Earth*.[15]

True to the sense of enigma that pervades the work, the pastor reverses himself completely and the text even suggests (Duncan never goes beyond suggestion) a new and surprising complicity between the Pukumina priestess, Mama Bull, and the pastor: "—It looks like the pastor and Mama Bull are getting along quite well ... —one of them said finally. —So it does ..." (p. 184). This exchange is immediately followed by a paragraph outlining the radically new stance taken by the pastor. He has now begun to preach over and over a "sermón sin sentido" (a sermon without meaning) that rings out with strong reminiscences of the Biblical prophet Isaiah: "'From among my people I will raise up one—says the Lord—I will take away his heart of stone and give him one of flesh, and he will be the liberation of many and the glory of the people.'" (The expression "peace of the people" originates in the same Biblical context). The people go to the Pukumina priestess for an explanation of this text in such a context, and her answer, fraught with the dramatic professionalism of the medium, is relatively lucid: "The priestess was silent for some moments, and then, rubbing a stone she had in her hands, she said that the answer lay in the midday silence, because one day *Cuminá* would become incarnate in the people and would be the people themselves, and their altars would be superfluous" (p. 184). All of the terms of her pronouncement had already begun to acquire some intelligibility through the alchemy of Duncan's narrative art.

The synthesizing of the disparate threads into a tentative but inspiring pattern of meaning comes only on the final page. In the first place there are two declarations that solemnly reiterate the judgement of Pedro's consummate virility rendered by Mariot and Perez. Then follows this paragraph, the longest and clearly the most important on the page, that is worth quoting in its entirety:

> The men did not wait for anything else. They immediately understood the pastor's insistent preaching, and were sure that he himself did not ever understand what he was saying. And they saw in all clarity, in the deep silence of the early morning, the noontime silence. (*Cuminá* danced the peace of the people). (p. 187)

The incomprehensible sermon and the enigmatically couched explanation by Mama Bull become crystal clear once the absolutely final judgment of Pedro's virility has been made. He is the man who will free his people from their oppression: he is the rebel par excellence. The metaphor chosen by the author through the vehicle of his pastor character is that of Pedro as messiah. The full understanding of this aspect of Pedro's role comes about, as Mama Bull had predicted, "in the profound silence of the early morning, the noontime silence." Furthermore, the final image contained in parentheses above is meant to express all of the elements of the essential metaphor: Pedro brings peace to his people, that is, he fulfills his role as messiah, in and through ritual possession by *Cuminá* during the trance induced by dance. This singularly syncretic image connects the core of Christianity, the religion that came via Europe, to the core of the Afro-folk religion developed in Jamaica. The true peace of the people is achieved not only through the process represented by the complex metaphor, but indeed through the metaphor itself for its creation rests on a familiarity with two cultural systems, it represents an act of creative syncretism.

This fundamental syncretism is a West Indian manifestation of a general Afro-American—"American" in the full sense of the term—phenomenon, and is presented in essentially similar terms in an earlier work, "La rebelión pocomía" (The Pukumina Rebellion). In that work the main character, a rebel inspired by possession by *Cuminá*, is Jean Paul, a descendant of Francophone West Indians. He too proposed strike action, he is seen in part as a Biblical figure—in his case it is John the Baptist. He too has Mama Bull as his spiritual mother in the Pukumina religion, and he too is the "horse" that Kumina mounts to dance. Jean Paul's revolutionary activities are short-lived, ending in definitive tragedy as he is shot down, according to tradition, by black folks in the pay of the oppressors. "La rebelión pocomía," then, published in 1976, contains the undeveloped germ of the novel that was to appear two years later. Duncan's experimentation with syncretism as an essential creative force in his art can thus be clearly documented. Charles McForbes as character is basically a product of this syncretic creativity, but it is with Pedro Dull that the author reaches the highpoint of the process.

The Conflict

The conditions in the real world that foster syncretism are the same that give rise to conflict which thus, in reality as well as artistically, is the other side of the coin. Obeah and Kumina, it is clear, are practices which conflict with many of the established beliefs and customs of the dominant groups in Caribbean societies. They are also important aspects of the West Indian folk milieu in which Duncan was raised. It is not surprising, therefore, that he has woven these elements artistically into the fabric of his fiction. The resultant conflict, it must be noted, defines the essential relationships in the lives of both Charles McForbes and Pedro Dull, and is thus central to the characterization as well as the development of plot in two of Duncan's most important novels, *Los cuatro espejos* and *La paz del pueblo*.

The plot of *Los cuatros espejos* can be reduced to a match-up between two world views: the magical West Indian Weltanschauung of the folk from Limón as against the so-called scientific approach of the white/mestizo dominant group centered in San José, the capital. Charles McForbes is the most important point of contact between the two worlds, and is thus the centre of the conflict. So poignant is the presentation of this conflict that it argues for the existence in the implied author (and perhaps even in the author himself) of a correspondingly intense inner turmoil: an argument that is strengthened by the fact that, as we shall point out later, there is no real solution offered.

The title of the work is a clear indication of its essential sense, and the four mirrors refer to the four occasions in the novel on which Charles looks into a mirror in a hugely symbolic effort at self-analysis, indeed in a desperate quest to find himself literally. The novel opens with the main character stricken by the most extreme psychological trauma when upon awakening one morning he finds that he cannot see his face, or more precisely he cannot see the exact color of his face, in the mirror.[16] Apparently this trauma was induced by a lecture on racism he attended the night before at the prestigious *Teatro Nacional*. It had touched home in every respect, for Charles was by this time comfortably ensconced in the lap of the white/mestizo national bourgeoisie, having won the hand of the daughter of one of the country's leading physicians. Of the three other attempts to find himself in the mirror, only the last one is successful; and this occurs after his Orphic descent to the land of his roots: his return to his past. Charles's identity crisis such as it is presented through the metaphor of the mirror is sociopsychological. However, it is very clear that it is initiated by the death of his first wife, the only woman he loved completely, Lorena. Her death functions in the plot both as catalyst and as condition *sine qua non* for bringing Charles's two worlds into sharp conflict.

The author clearly intends the circumstances surrounding Lorena's death to be a test of strength of the two opposing world views. After the fateful attack on Lorena by a particularly daring duppy, "un fantasma blanco, descarado," Charles balks at accepting the clear reality of the options open to him: "It was hard to accept so magical a solution after so much exposure to study." And the author adds immediately with a touch of wry self-mocking humour: "Although it wasn't that much after all" (p. 41). Right into this situation the champion of science makes her "súbita" (sudden) appearance. She is Clarita de Duke, the white/mestizo wife of one of the West Indians, and she is, to boot, a nurse, the most exalted representative of the scientific community in the village. Taking her calling with utmost seriousness, she sweeps in upon the scene and attempts to impose the scientific point of view: "With one single look she dismantled the basis of their cosmogony; a challenging, authoritarian look" (p. 42). The author states quite plainly that the crux of the matter was that there were two worlds in face-to-face confrontation: "Because they were two irreconcilable worlds, each one with its own logic" (p. 42). It would take more than the brash self-confidence of a country nurse to topple the edifice of the West Indian folk beliefs, and Clarita's pretensions are rejected flatly after a moment's hesitation, when someone affirms that "instead of injections she needed an obeah man" (p. 42).

The sense of confrontation intensifies later on when, either in a dream or a vision (this detail is typically left unclear), Charles's father (now deceased) appears to Lorena advising her that the source of her misfortune is some white powder placed under a large flowerpot. She immediately summons Charles to her sickbed and enjoins: "—Put lime on your hands and remove the powder right now. You have to do it right away" (p. 51). The lime is a well-known antidote against magical toxicity. Again Charles finds himself torn between the two worlds within him. His studies impel him to reject all the superstitious nonsense, but his culture indicates to him quite clearly that the phenomena he is really experiencing are certain proof of the validity of so-called superstitious practices. The dilemma is described in these terms: "It was a terrible moment. Suddenly his twenty-three years came together—including the years of secondary school and of studying theology—concentrating past and present into that moment" (p. 51). He yields to his wife's injunctions, and in fact does find the powder in the spot indicated. Still looking for the logical, scientific explanation, "His years of secondary school told him that it was a suggestion, a strong mental suggestion," he himself begins to see visions: "the sudden apparition of an ethereal being resembling his father ... the later apparition of another being resembling Jakel Duke" —Jakel Duke, like his father, is now deceased. It is finally these two "ghosts" who determine the course of action that Charles will follow: "Both explained to him that with the help of a doctor Lorena could prolong her life a little, but that the damage was already done and it was too late now" (p. 52).

Charles takes his wife to the hospital in the capital, and her case attracts the interest of the nation's leading physician, Lucas Centeno, who becomes Charles's friend and counsellor, and finally his father-in-law. Lorena's lingering illness baffles the medical establishment, and, fulfilling the prophesy of the other-worldly visitors, she succumbs after a year. The brash self-confidence that generally characterizes the scientific community is reduced to the following admission of impotence from the lips of one of its most outstanding representatives, Dr. Centeno: "'The fact is that I know what you have and I cannot cure you. Yes, I know very well what you have, my black friend. But I cannot cure you. Or perhaps, that's not what you have ...', and he went into a fit of distraction, staring off into space" (p. 87). Total incoherence is all that the eminent doctor can offer to Lorena.

The same kind of conflict had been presented in a almost the same terms in an earlier short story, "La luz del vigía," (The Signalman's Light) from Quince Duncan's first collection, *Una canción en la madrugada* (1970).[17] In this work it is a local school teacher who champions the cause of science in the face of her pupils' respectful fear inspired by the phenomenon of a strange light that would appear at night on the railroad tracks close by the spot on which a signalman had met an untimely death. Like Clarita de Duke, the local school teacher imposes her intellectual-moral authority, declaring flatly: "I have fought against superstition in the classroom, now I have the opportunity to do so in the very place where these things you have all imagined took place" (p. 54). She and her band of newly made converts to the scientific point of view set off to confront the ghostly light that very night. They try to catch up with the light but it eludes them, dancing to and fro as it disappears and reappears mockingly. The story ends with these telling sentences: "Sad, with bowed heads, overcome and meditative, each one set out for his home, drinking the bitter dregs of defeat. They trod underfoot scientific omniscience and the whole legion of its apostles" (p. 56).

The conflict between the scientific approach and the magical one such as it is presented in *Los cuatro espejos* and "La luz del vigía" is mostly an ideological one of opposing world views. In *La paz del pueblo*, as in "La rebelión pocomía," however, it is presented in its full socioeconomic and political dimensions. In both novels the conflict is artistically developed through the death of the important female protagonist, and, of course, in both the male protagonist serves as the imporant vehicle through which the religious theme is introduced. As was pointed out in the case of Charles McForbes, Duncan uses both the

syncretic and the conflictive mode in the elaboration of the pivotal religious theme. The same is true for *La paz del pueblo's* Pedro Dull, for it is through him that the revolutionary (i.e. conflictive) aspect of Afro-folk religion is manifested. He is on the one hand the epitome of the spirit of radical liberation in the Judeo-Christian tradition, being a messiah figure. On the other hand, as an embodiment of *Cuminá*, he is a forceful representative of the Afro-American revolutionary religious tradition. This latter, a perennial tradition, has engendered such phenomena as the voodoo-inspired Haitian Revolution, the Morant Bay Rebellion in Jamaica, and the contemporary Black Power movement in the United States.[18] What is true for Pedro is true also for Jean Paul, his forerunner in Duncan's fictional universe.

The Samamfo

The distinction between the tolerance/syncretic and the conflictive aspects of the religious experience is a useful analytical tool, but one that functions like a scaffold and that is thus frequently outstripped by the development of the analysis. Such was the case not only in our treatment of Duncan's characters but also in our exploration of such concepts as "Kumina,'" "obeah," and "Pukumina," which could all be appreciated or studied in accordance with either of the two modes. In the matter of the *samamfo* the distinction is considerably less helpful, and, therefore, our analysis, while building on it, has essentially evolved past it.

The *samamfo* makes its initial appearance in the early part of *La paz del pueblo* in a fragment of conversation between an unidentified grandfather and his grandchild, equally unidentified:

—Grandfather and ...how does this business about heaven and hell go?

—That is when it's all over. At the end, after the judgment. But for now nobody dies, son: we simply return to the *samamfo*. (p. 24)

This is an excellently conceived theological exposition within the traditional West African mode. It is entirely consistent with all of the principles of African philosophy and religions enunciated by such writers as Alexis Kagame, Janheinz Jahn, John S. Mbiti, and others, for it celebrates vitality, life after death, and the interrelationship between the spirit world beyond death—the world of the "living dead"—and that of the living.[19] Above all, it conforms fully to the formal definition of *"samamfo"* that Duncan gives in his glossary to *La paz del pueblo*: "a word of Ashanti origin which signifies the place or state in which the dead find themselves, or the spirits of the ancestors" (p. 192).[20]

Duncan presents the *samamfo* as more than just a consciousness actualized in the minds of certain characters and in that of the narrator and implied author. It is rather a dynamic living presence that activates all beings, maintaining a constructive continuity between them. In *La paz del pueblo*, for example, the important background character, Señora Mariot, undertakes as a young girl an act of rebellion that is the direct result of this *samamfo* force: "That was the reason for her decision. Counseled by who knows what hidden forces of the *samamfo*, which made her capable of the supreme act of rebellion" (p. 132). The affirmation of her independence brought her to Limón from Jamaica after fleeing from her aunt's repressive tutelage. It prefigures Pedro's future revolt that constitutes the central element of the plot. The author clearly intends to make a definite connection between the two acts of rebellion, for the older woman, who always, more so than any other character, attends to the promptings of the *samamfo*, gives herself to Pedro—her daughter, Sitaira's, lover—and this act is itself given special significance. A context is created in which central mention is made of the *samamfo* in the two paragraphs leading up to the description of Mariot's offer of herself to Pedro. In each of these two paragraphs the last words are in fact: "...inheritor of the *samamfo*," and, "... the glory of the *samamfo*," respectively. Then the act is pointedly painted in these terms: "You will remember her, her convulsions, the joy with which she gave herself, her fanatical fidelity to the *samamfo*, the final spasm and then the casual remark: 'I'm old now, but maybe ...'" (p. 169). To intensify even further the highly charged account, Duncan takes liberties with the normal logic of tense use. He recounts a past action—a recollection—in the future tense. This technique reminds the reader immediately of a work like Carlos Fuentes' *La muerte de Artemio Curz* (1961), one of the best known of the "boom" novels.[21] Obviously the suggestion contained in Mariot's final direct words amounts to a desperately unrealistic plea for some sort of permanent relationship with the young man who had been her deceased daughter's lover. The reader is left with a strong sense of the force of the *samamfo* and of its extraordinary importance in the relationship between Pedro and Señora Mariot.

It is in Duncan's latest published short story, "Los mitos ancestrales," that the concept of the *samamfo* attains its fullest stature as a base for fiction.[22] This story is a remarkably symbolic tale recounting allegorically the history of colonization in Africa. Somewhat similar to the kind of creativity that Cubena practices, Duncan attempts to reconstruct an African mythology based on his erudite familiarity with African philosophy and religions. The style is experimental with some degree of surrealism, and indeed large doses of all of the narrative techniques that Spanish American writers have in recent times taken great delight in using. The principal character and first-person narrator is an inhabitant of the *samamfo*, and hence the setting is the world of the living dead. This immediately recalls the situation in Juan Rulfo's *Pedro Páramo* (1955), a novel constructed entirely on the actions of characters who, it turns out, have all already died. There are clear reminiscences too of *Palace of the Peacock* (1960) by the Guyanese novelist Wilson Harris.[23] Of course, Duncan's approach is fully consistent with the concept of the *samamfo*, and one would have to conclude that it is inspired more by African philosophy than by his reading of Rulfo—he is entirely unfamiliar with Harris's work.[24] The main character is assigned these lines: "And they executed us both, my valiant son and myself, in the public square, on the fifth day when to my embarrassment the week began on a Monday" (p. 81), clearly establishing his beyond-this-world status.

In this story even more so than in *La paz del pueblo*, the sacred principles of the *samamfo* govern all of the actions of the characters, necessarily so. The narrative constantly brings this out; for example, on the opening page recalling the glories of the precolonial past this sentence occurs: "And that night we gave thanks to *Nyambe* (2) and to the *Samamfo* (3) for the benefits given to all the families of the territory" (p. 73). Duncan explains in footnotes that Nyambe is God for the Ashantis and also defines *Samamfo* as "spirit and inheritance of the ancestors." In accordance with this basic formulation, colonization is seen as an abandonment of the principles of the *Samamfo*. When at the end of his extraordinarily complex tale the main character reviews his infidelities to these sacred principles, he makes the following observation: "History will say that I abandoned her for a silver woman. And it will say that at the end of my days I reneged on my golden dreams. It will say that I have betrayed the most sacred element of the *Samamfo*" (p. 90). "Silver" is associated with the white colonizer's world, and "gold" represents the pristine values of the African world. Here the symbolism touches on a theme that was important in *Los cuatro espejos*, namely, the sociological implications of interracial amorous relationships. For at the end of his long and very active revolutionary and counterrevolutionary life the main character seems to have opted for the world of "silver" and the corresponding female for whom, it may appear, he abandoned his African wife.

Nothing, however, is certain in Duncan's universe except the general principles. This is precisely the understanding on which the main character bases his ultimate vindication of the vicissitudes with which his career has been fraught: "But I have told the tale of the *Samamfo*. I alone. I have adored *Nyambe* and I have made him incarnate in the People" (p. 91). Whatever may be said about the validity of this justification of personal and public infidelities, it is clearly an assertion of the importance of the *Samamfo* not only as a guiding principle for action, but indeed as a dynamic reality in its own right. Furthermore, the terms in which the main character articulates his relationship to God, *Nyambe*, are essentially the same as those in which Duncan expresses Pedro's fidelity to *Cuminá*: "... I have made him incarnate in the People."

There is depth as well as consistency in the philosophical base on which Duncan constructs his fictional universe. Religious thought appears to be the essence of this base, and this religious thought is demonstrably as much African as it is European. Nothing ever seems to be definitively resolved in Duncan's universe. Charles McForbes perhpas settles down to a stable self-fulfilling life. Pedro's attainment of the fullest measure of manhood through fidelity to *Cuminá* may foster some degree of greater political freedom and socioeconomic well-being for his people. At least it did not lead to his immediate physical death as was the case with his forerunner, Jean Paul. The main character is "Los mitos ancestrales" has perhaps justified himself in spite of the appearances and is perhaps worthy of his place in the *samamfo*. Duncan's contribution lies not in the solutions he provides but rather in the questions he poses and the terms in which addresses them. His work stands as a source of sustenance for West Indian culture, giving expression to the religious roots of this culture and to the twin processes of syncretism and conflict that constitute its essential dynamic—and indeed the essential creative dynamic in the author himself. It is through the religious theme that this West Indian culture is given coherence in Duncan's universe.

Some West Indian Themes: The Plantation, Interracial Love, The Journey

Duncan's real-life situation makes him acutely aware of the presence of the plantation in the lives of West Indian Costa Ricans, and this awareness is actualized in his works. In his novels the central idea of both the plot and the characterization process assumes the persistence of the plantation as an active force. For, as we have seen, the essential action in *La paz del pueblo* revolves around Pedro's struggle to free himself and his people from the oppressive elements of the plantation. The society in which Pedro and all of the characters live and move is an authentic plantation society. The same is obviously true for the world depicted in the short story "La rebelión pocomía." In *Los cuatro espejos* the plantation can be considered to be much more elaborately conceived. The essential confrontation it presents between the Afro-Caribbean and the white/mestizo Costa Rican worlds can be seen as a clash between the plantation society and the metropolis, or more precisely between the undisguised plantation society and a surrogate metropolis that is really itself a watered down version of the plantation. Certainly the relationship between San José, the capital, and the province of Limón, the Afro-Antillean world, is presented in these terms.

Thus the novel's protagonist, Charles, is representative of all colonized men. He himself gives voice in the most direct fashion to the basic nature of his dilemma: "I ended up a prisoner of both worlds, trapped between two cultures..." (p. 153). The two worlds he refers to are defined and distinguishable, not exclusively but all the same in a very basic sense, on the basis of the plantation concept. In the terms developed in the chapter on language, Charles's problem is one of trying to follow the Flexibility-Synthesis model in a society which imposes the Conflict-Replacement model. This is precisely one of the frames of reference that Duncan, the author and thinker, uses to focus on the essential problem of the colonized man. In "Los mitos ancestrales," a story which presents one of the most impressive metaphorical dramatizations of the colonial process, the epigraph is from A. Sivanandan: "On the margin of European culture ... the 'coloured' intellectual is an artifact of colonial history ... He is a creature of two worlds, and of none" (p. 73). Sivanandan's idea has greatly impressed Duncan, it is the same idea contained in the crucial lines from *Los cuatro espejos* that were quoted earlier: "Because they were two irreconcilable worlds, each one with its own logic" (p. 42).

The immediate context of Charles's cry of distress was the serious personal conflict occasioned by his involvement with Engracia, a white/mestizo woman with whom he was having an affair. This affair itself prefigures his marriage to Ester, a white/mestizo woman who is as well a solid member of the capital's upper class. In addition, the affair with Engracia undermines his commitment to his native world after Lorena's death. Not only does Charles marry Ester, but he has a previous affair with Ester's cousin, also white/mestizo and very bourgeois. The person who championed the cause of science right after the fateful duppy attack on Lorena, Clarita de Duke, is a white/mestizo woman who is married to Clif Duke, an Afro-Antillean. Duncan is keenly aware of the racism that pervades the entire Costa Rican society, and he discusses it frankly and intelligently throughout the novel, and indeed throughout his work. However, whereas interracial sex is a significant fact in that it occasions and symbolizes unspeakable sociological and psychological problems, it is not seen in itself as unreachable and a pervasive preoccupation of black males. in fact, fact, quite a commonplace occurence—as the examples cited above help to demonstrate. This approach to the subject, as was indicated in the later pages of Chapter One, is characteristic of the black writer in contrast to the white one.

Both the theme of the plantation and that of interracial sex reflect the realities of life for most West Indian Costa Ricans. Furthermore, the plantation theme is one that pervades all other Caribbean literatures, and it has been contended in Chapter One of this book that the theme of interracial sex is one of the most important in Afro-Spanish American literature.

It is with the theme of the journey that the most explicit bonds of communality are set up with the other Caribbean literatures. This theme, according to George Lamming, one of the leading contemporary novelists from the Caribbean, is fundamental both in his work and in that of his fellow Caribbean authors. All the major Caribbean works, in Lamming's view, are stories of a voyage of some type. He identifies various phases in the journey metaphor: the original journey, Columbus, the Middle Passage, etc; the migration from a rural to an urban environment, depicted in such novels as *Jane's Career* (1914) and *The Harder They Come* (1980) by the Jamaicans H. G. De Lisser and Michael Thelwell respectively, as well as *La Rue cases-nègres*

(1950) by the Martinican Joseph Zobel; the interior journey, the problem of self-realization, as in *Minty Alley* (1936), *A Brighter Sun* (1952), and *A House for Mr. Biswas* (1961) by the Trinidadians C. L. R. James, Samuel Selvon, and V. S. Naipaul respectively; the journey into new exile in the metropolitan centers, as in the Afro-American novel *Native Son* (1940) by Richard Wright or in Selvon's *The Lonely Londoners* (1956); finally there is the journey of reaffirmation, the journey back to Africa, either real or symbolic. This phase is best treated in Edward Brathwaite's poetry.[25] Gregory Urban Rigsby, a West Indian critic, sees the theme of the "mystic quest" as the shaping factor in Caribbean literature: "Caribbean literature is, therefore, to a large extent 'quest literature.'"[26]

Charles McForbes made several journeys back and forth between the two worlds before undertaking the most important one, the Orphic journey into his past and into his native world to seek liberation from his trauma. This final journey constitutes one of the pillars of the novel's plot, and it represents the final stage of the archetypal journey outlined by Lamming, namely, the return of reaffirmation. Charles, like Jane of *Jane's Career*, Jose Hassam of *La Rue cases-nègres*, and Ivan of *The Harder They Come*, had already undertaken the "journey within" from country to town. In Charles's case this was also a journey from plantation to semimetropolis. He had also, like Tiger in *A Brighter Sun* and Mr. Biswas in *A House for Mr. Biswas*, completed the "interior journey" of self-realization, rising above the limits of his original immediate socioeconomic circumstances.

In *La paz del pueblo* the most basic stage of the journey symbol is given resonance for the action of the work includes scenes set in Jamaica, the second *terminus a quo*. The new "middle passage" from Jamaica to Central America is presented as an important aspect of the novel's context. La señora Mariot has, in fact, lived through both experiences: life in Jamaica and the new "passage," coming to establish herself in the "new world" of Limón. She is the vehicle par excellence for the elaboration of the basic journey metaphor. Pedro is also a voyager in the fullest sense of the term. He is an outsider who comes upon the scene, acts out his role, decides to make a tactical retreat from the village to avoid unjust prosecution, but changes his mind and returns. It is a precarious return, however, for he comes back to imprisonment and the possible extinction of his dreams. So it is neither a return to the native land nor even a return to fulfillment, but Duncan clearly establishes that the decision to return is itself an act of the highest merit, the ultimate demonstration of Pedro's manhood.

The concept of language as a West Indian theme has already been treated in the preceding chapter. The important trio: identity, race, and protest, whose heuristic potential was incontrovertibly evinced in Rex Nettleford's *Identity Race and Protest in Jamaica,* has been shown in the course of this chapter to be relevant to the discussion of Quince Duncan's work. The themes are enshrined in the author's approach to the question of religion with his abiding fidelity to the basic sense of independence and self-realization of the folk religions practiced by the Africans who came to constitute the mass of Jamaica's population. Exile, one of the important recurring themes in all Caribbean literature, is obviously related to and can be subsumed under our discussion of the theme of the journey. In all of its basic aspects then of form and content, Duncan's fictional universe is holistically West Indian, unlike the fictional universes of the non-West Indian authors who have been referred to as "precursors."

CHAPTER FOUR

CUBENA'S WEST INDIAN RAGE

The following lines from Emerson stand as the epigraph to Cubena's first publication, *Cuentos del negro Cubena* (Short Stories by Cubena the Black) (1977): "The man is only half himself,/the other half is his expression."[1] From the very onset Cubena has clearly declared his literary endeavour, his art, to be an assertion of complete selfhood. It will turn out to be a vociferous assertion of a self that is West Indian, in fact, an unequivocal proclamation of the selfhood of the entire Afro-Antillean Panamanian people. This chapter will show how the proclamation and the sense of outrage that accompanies it constitute the most salient of the cluster of features that make up the "West Indianness" of Cubena's universe. The "West Indianness" is itself the hub of this universe, for it is central not only to the structure and characterization but to other elements of Cubena's creativity, corresponding to those that this book has already singled out for study in the other authors.

Cubena has written so far two prose works: his collection of short stories cited above, and a novel, *Chombo* (1981).[2] In addition, he has published a slim volume of poems, *Pensamientos del negro Cubena* (Cubena the Black's Thoughts) (1977).[3] The novel will be the main point of reference in this present chapter with some mention being made of the *Cuentos*.

"Chombo" Selfhood Proclaimed

History and the Structure of Chombo

With the publication of *Chombo* it has become clear that Cubena is interested in creating through his narrative a fictional universe whose different parts coalesce into one coherent structure. The basis of this coherence is the reappearance in fuller bloom of the characters from the *Cuentos*. Analogous to Balzac's *"comédie humaine,"* Cubena's fictional universe will chronicle the West Indian residence in Panama. The clearest indication of this artistic purpose is the apparent establishing of the entire Afro-Antillean people as the protagonist of his novel.

The very title "*Chombo*" is a brilliantly conceived expression of Cubena's intent. It clearly connotes a chronicle of the experience of the entire people. It goes further, however, since it is also an exclamation and a defiant declaration. The term is normally used pejoratively, and the utterance itself, "*chombo*" (masculine singular form without the article), because of its morphological characteristics is made in the context of a face-to-face situation in which someone is being called "*chombo*." Now the Spanish masculine singular form can stand for both men and women in a generalized sense. So "*chombo*" is the form used for hurling an insult at the entire group. This is the form that Cubena chooses as his title. By so doing he has taken advantage of all of its violent energy, and, with an act of his sovereign will as the recipient and thus the generator of this explosive force, he has re-directed it back against those who channelled it towards him. He is like the brave soldier who catches a hand grenade in midair and hurls it back against his attackers. So the explosive force of "*chombo!*" now bursts in the very faces of the would-be assailants. The title *Chombo* most aptly, then, conveys the very sense of the novel, an affirmation of the peoplehood of the Panamanians of Anglophone Caribbean ancestry, along with an expression of intense outrage at the racist assaults against that very peoplehood.

This interpretation is further enhanced by careful consideration of the full sense of the first page, the dedication page. With characteristic directness the author states simply: "Dedicatoria: A mi gente" (Dedication: To my people). Both of his prior books had been dedicated in the first instance to two particular representatives of his people, Papa James and Nenen, individuals to whom he, the author, owed an individual and significant debt. But in each case Cubena's dedication moved on to a more universal plane. In the *Cuentos* he mentions as well "all persons of African ancestry," and in the *Pensamientos*, along with Papa James and Nenen, his dedication includes "all lovers of PEACE, LOVE, JUSTICE." The vision has become firmly fixed in *Chombo*, because in view of the strong sense of the title the "gente" (of the dedication) can only be *los chombos*, his fellow Panamanians of Anglophone Caribbean ancestry.

The epigraph in *Chombo* is also different from that used in both the *Cuentos* and the *Pensamientos*. Now that Cubena has firmly established that his art is a proclamation of selfhood, this novel, his first of a trilogy that he has promised, will proudly proclaim the selfhood of the *chombos*. The epigraph from Marcus Garvey confirms this: "A people without the knowledge of their past history, origin and culture is like a tree without roots." Following strictly the admonition contained in these words of a prophetic black leader—the most influential in this century, and perhaps in all centuries—Cubena will structure his novel so as to be the most effective root for the tree of his people.

The structure that indeed emerges in *Chombo* is one that most suitably gives expression and stands as a monument to the history, origin, and culture of a specific group of black people: a group that is solidly presented as a branch of the firmly rooted tree. The approach chosen has, of course, the grave inherent danger of yielding a structure that is too diffuse to be artistically sound. For such an approach is best served by the creation of a plethora of personas, even some from the land of the dead. It takes all of Cubena's artistic skill to mold his historical elements into a meaningful and tasteful mosaic. It takes all of his talent to keep the novel from descending into a diatribe on the history of the race.[4]

The question of history is directly addressed in a charactersitically brief introductory letter to the readers. It contains just two short paragraphs which each contain a key concept. The first acknowledges that the novel "is pregnant with historical data and anecdotes about black West Indians—chombos."[5] Cubena's words are especially significant because they contain an explicit reference to and thus justification of the title of the novel—much more explicit than anything in the text of the work itself. The novel will be a history of the "chombos." The second key concept contained in the second paragraph is a well-derived corollary of the first. Cubena expresses it thus: "In the reading that you are about to undertake, you will encounter the reasons that make it necessary and above all URGENT to combat the pernicious racial discrimination and other injustices...." Exposure to the history of the "chombos" elicits an immediate response; the author has proclaimed this history and encoded his response in the very title. The introductory letter then confirms this interpretation.

The novel's title fully interlocks with its structure to express with coherent symbolism the author's apparent major message. The characterization process fits harmoniously into the pattern. *Chombo* chronicles the life histories of a number of representative *chombos* giving them existence in fiction and thus selfhood, in accordance with the Emersonian saying: "The man is only half himself. The other half is his expression." Litó, the more or less main character, is, then, literally but one of a crowd. Besides making him a fictionalized version of himself, Cubena, true to his manifest purpose, has done little to develop the character.

Litó enters the fictional world in a violent rage. The very opening words of the novel are his: "—Carajo! Me ca ..." (Damn! Sh...). Then the narrator comments, making sure that the point is not missed: "At the very moment he was vomiting up these inner thoughts that from time immemorial had burned at the furious young black man's ulcerous innards ...," (p. 9). Rage and disgust are the dominant sentiments, and the very word "vomiting" is especially significant for, in fact, Cubenà will use this most obvious symbol throughout his work as an adequate expression of his and his characters' reaction to the injustices of racism. Litó's rage persists through the entire novel, and he will exit the scene in an equally impressive burst of violent rage. The penultimate chapter of the book ends with his awakening suddenly from an uneasy sleep he had fallen into on a train ride back to Panama City. He had had a dream, but a dream of violent vengeance wreaked on the white oppressor. Upon awakening he adopts the position of a *capoeira* (an African form of martial arts practiced in Brazil) fighter. The narrator continues: "The young black man was fed up to the teeth with this business of racial discrimination and injustices. He was furious" (p. 96). The chapter ends a few lines later with an intense outburst of emotion that is not only briefly expressed but dramatically so, for the sentence ends with an ellipsis: "Then, with his fist he began squashing white cockroaches, white rats, white dogs ..." (p. 96). The obvious symbolism is quite intentional and has been sustained throughout the book.

Litó's early life history is not recounted until the second half of the novel. He is the son of Nenen's adopted daughter Abena Mansa Adesimbo. The viciously brutal circumstances in which he was conceived are recounted with an equally brutal starkness: "And at five o'clock sharp in the evening just after taking her leave of Leonora Dehaney, in a narrow alleyway lit only by the sad whiteness of the moon, Abena Mansa Adesimbo was raped by a mulatto. He was the son of the West Indian neighbours who were frequently drunk" (p. 57). Immersed in the penury and promiscuity that were the lot of many of Panama's *chombos*, Litó and his two siblings, Chabela and Turo, all fathered in similar dehumanizing violence, become examples of survival and success against the overwhelming odds. In this respect, his function is fundamental to Cubena's didactic intent summed up in the motto emblazoned on his chosen coat of arms: "Ebeyiye" (The future will be better).[6] His role in the novel is fundamental in other respects as well. It is his quest for the alluringly significant family hierloom, three gold bracelets, that provides the novel's central action. Furthermore, his reflections on the situation of *chombos* in particular and black people in general give rise to many of the narrator's didactic pronouncements. All indications are that Cubena wishes to identify with the narrator.

The other characters of *Chombo* can be divided into three basic categories: the ordinary folk who, in fact, made up the vast majority of the migrants to Panama, then those among the masses who stood out for some particular reason, and finally the symbolic ancestors. Nenen and Papa James are the most important of the ordinary folks. Their story is told in the third chapter, "*Yawoada*," by "the oldest African ancestor" in order to explain "the matter of the three gold bracelets" (p. 33). The information or vision comes to Litó one idyllic tropical morning as he sits in the shade of a mango tree poring over his notes "taken from articles written by Dr. George Westerman, and others by Professor Armando Fortune on the black man's contribution to the culture and enonomy of the isthmus of Panama. Besides, to get ready for the first Congress of Black Culture in the Americas that was to take place in Cali, Colombia he had begun to read a most important study on the black West Indian written by Roy S. Bryce-Laporte, one of Panama's eminent sociologists" (p. 32). There is a relatively large slice of real life thus introduced into this work of fiction, and precisely at the point at which the oldest of the African ancestors from the Kingdom of the Dead is going to intervene. This circumstance serves to heighten greatly the importance of the communication from the ancestor: the telling of the life histories of James Duglin, Nenen, and a number of West Indian migrants. The commuication will continue throughout the next two chapters, "*Efiada*" and "*Memeneda*," Chapters Three and Four, and occupy a significant portion of the novel.

A pattern emerges from the proliferation of biographical data, for they all amount to elements of the vicious cycle of African slavery in the New World. In the first place all the characters left a mythical homeland, Xaymaca-Nokoro, to go to Panama. This allows the narrator to dwell on the repeated symbolism of the Middle Passage and the importance of ships in the history of all black people in the Americas. The ships in *Chombo* are the *Waterloo* and the *Telémaco*, names pregnant with ominous symbolism of crushed hopes and of the tortuous trial of quest for long-lost loved ones. These ships are materially and chronologically different from the slave ships, but their purpose and effect are essentially similar. Hard labor under horrendous conditions is the lot of the new "slaves," as the quickly told stories of the tribulations of the migrants on the *Telémaco* forcefully reveal: Leonora Dehaney, Cuffee, Kingstonboy, Bouckman, Calpyso Joe, Tidam Frenchí, the names are different but the circumstances are exactly the same. The new masters are the racist agents of North Atlantic capitalist imperialism, aptly symbolized by the odious Huncle Zam (Cubena is rather clever with the use of names, as we shall see later). The only alternative to the degrading and life-destroying labor on the Canal Zone is the equally degrading and potentially life-destroying, and perhaps even more sordid, existence in the ghettos of Panama City, beleagured by the petty persecutions of "lesser" *latino* racists, symbolized by the members of the Simeñíquez and Barrescoba clans. They are buffeted too by their own pettiness and fratricidal strife as exemplified in the absurdly destructive struggle between Nenen and Tidam Frenchi that led to the demise of their sidewalk vending business, and to the success of their Italian and Chinese rivals.

In this hateful exile, return to Xaymaca-Nokoró is the chief source of consolation. It is Papa James's constant preoccupation. However, old age and death snatch him away amidst his dreams and plans. Nenen's case is even more pathetic, for her death comes at the very moment when the longed for return is a realizable reality: the ticket has been purchased, the bags have been packed, and the passport has been issued. Consistent with his didactic intent Cubena makes the point very clearly that escape is not a viable option, as the facts of history indicate that the only solution is the reconstruction of a meaningful existence, turning exile into commitment. Thus Litó, Chabela, and Turo after three long generations of struggle come to make something of their lives, becoming a professor, a nurse, and a physician respectively.

Cubena as narrator and "griot" must concern himself above all with the heroes of the people, those whom the tribe recognizes as having special merit. In the case of the *chombos* such heroes are usually either unsung or directly calumniated by the rest of the society. Thus, among the many West Indians who died of yellow fever and malaria during the construction of the canal, mention is made of "the case of Accompong and Quaco, defenders of just causes, they died in the revolutionary conflict led by Pedro Prestán the mulatto, who, for trying to liberate Colon City from the Yankee yoke, was hanged along with the Haitian Antonio Pautrizelle and the Jamaican George Davis better known as Cocobolo" (p. 39). Tidam Frenchí, while she instructs her two daughters in the fine art of sewing, inculcates in them a sense of their roots by telling them of her native lands, Haiti and St. Lucia. Then the narrator/griot continues: "However, her favorite theme was that of the feats of the Martinican maroon leader Francisque Fabule; and especially the celebrated maroon woman Zabeth from Haiti. At times she recounted details about *Le Maniel*, the most famous of the Haitian maroon strongholds; about the routing of the Napoleonic troops in Haiti; and about the Haitians who fought along with Simon Bolivar for the liberation of the South American countries" (p. 53). Here again the history lesson and the fictive element become indistinguishable, in perfect accord with the concept of fiction that Cubena has decided to adopt.

More intimately connected with the fictional edifice of this particular novel is the case of Papa James's problems with the Canal Zone authorities. He is deported from the Zone, an affront to his Panamanian nationality, especially since this absurd situation of being barred from entering an area of the national territory by the authorities of a foreign nation has been decreed to be "In Perpetuity." The narrator continues: "And James Duglin's situation went from bad to worse because of his friendship for Samuel Inniss and his countryman William Preston Stoute, brave organizers of the strike by Canal Zone workers to protest racial discrimination and the injustice of the *Gold* and *Silver Roll*" (p. 55). Were it not for Cubena's writings these details of the history of West Indian Panamanians would have remained forever in some obscure corner of the history books, or would have enjoyed only the rich but culture specific and, for that reason, relatively limited life in the group's oral literature: folk tales, songs and sayings especially.

The third category of West Indian characters consists of the mythological prototypes of the *chombos*, the African ancestors. In this aspect of his art Cubena has complied with the primordial injunction of traditional African morality: that of honoring the ancestors, immediate as well as remote. Indeed the poet Edward Brathwaite has pointed disturbingly to the transgression for which all the Africans who survived the Middle Passage must acknowledge collective guilt. They have failed to duly honor their ancestors, for the ancestors of this group have in great measure been definitively forgotten, consigned to the depths of the cruel Middle-Passage sea. This is the basic wrong that the race of Africans resident in the Americas has to right.[7] Cubena in accordance with this view has undertaken the obligation of amending the evil, and, furthermore, paying particular attention to his immediate case. Consequently, the ancestors are explicitly and frequently summoned into Cubena's fictional universe where they play an important role, away from the darkness of uncaring oblivion. In this matter Cubena also displays a firm grasp of the fundamental principle of Bantu metaphysics as enunciated by Temples, Kagame, Jahn, and others: namely, that being is a vital force, *Ntu*.[8]

The three gold bracelets provide one of the fictional devices by which the mythical ancestors are made aesthetically relevant to the work. The bracelets are themselves a powerful symbol, for their meaning is founded on the acceptance of a pre-Columbian African presence in America. They are "precious gifts of the allies of the Onítefos [original Africans] in Cuzco, Chichen Itzá and Tenochtitlán" (p. 99). It is in the final chapter that the ancestor's life stories are told with the same schematic brevity that characterizes the telling of the life histories of the multitude of *chombos*. The integrally mythical quality of the narration is established immediately, for the opening paragraph reads: "One Tuesday at three o'clock sharp in the afternoon, close by a mango tree, a tortoise invited a spider and a serpent to hear his telling of the true and, above all, the complete story of the three gold bracelets. And he said:" (p. 97). In its brevity and intensity the paragraph is typical of Cubena, containing symbolic elements not only from the core personal symbolism that Cubena has developed, but also from the general symbolism evolved through the history of the race. Tuesday is the most important day of the week for Cubena, it is the day on which he was born and the day after which he takes his very nom de plume. The tortoise is an integral element of his coat of arms. The spider (Anancy) is the basic totemic creature in the philosophy and folklore of the Jamaican people, who are predominantly of Ashanti origin. The serpent figures in an equally fundamental fashion in the folklores and philosophies of many African (and indeed non-African peoples): from the Haitians—of Dahomean origin—with their Damballa, the snake *loa*, to the primordial Aztec myth of the eagle and the serpent (*el águila y la serpiente*).

The tortoise then assumes the role of narrator to tell the life history of the mythical ancestors. He begins at the very beginning "in *Abibiman* (Africa), three centuries after the birth of the first *onipa* (man)" (p. 97). As was indicated earlier, it was the ancestors themselves who told the life histories of the *chombos,* and so it is aesthetically most fitting that their life history should be recounted by the symbol of agelessness, the tortoise. The brief finale spans the entire history of the race, connecting the beginning in Africa to the beginning in the Americas. It is incidentally also a history of the white/albino man's inhumanity to man (fundamentally black), and the three gold bracelets provide one of the important linking devices. The story (and the novel) ends with the following two paragraphs:

> After the bloody massacre in Nokoró [the primordial village], when the surviving villagers were put in chains on board a slave ship under the command of an albino Christian captain, one of the Onítefo maidens managed to hide the three gold bracelets.
>
> Years later, the three gold bracelets reappeared in the maroon stronghold of Xayamaca-Nokoró on the banks of the Great River in Jamaica. And, after three centuries, the three gold bracelets reached Panama when the *Telémaco,* packed with black West Indians contracted to work on the construction of the Canal, dropped anchor in the port of Cristóbal en route from Kingston, Jamaica, where Nenen, one of the passengers, had found a little girl beside a dead woman descendant of the Onífeto clan, whose maroon African ancestors had founded Xaymaca-Nokoró." (pp. 99-100)

The massacre was perpetrated by a clan of congenitally malevolent albinos who had sprung up by some evil quirk of fate in the very bosom of the original race of founders of Nokoró. With these two paragraphs Cubena provides an impressively lucid denouement to his novel by repeating now, with the powerful fullness of the significance acquired over the evolution of the plot, the essential allegory, the summation of the mythically circular history of the *chombos*, a clearly defined branch on the deeply rooted and immensely extensive African family tree.

Rage and its Relief

In important aspects of its structure, namely, the title, the plot, and the characterization, the novel, *Chombo*, proclaims the peoplehood of the *chombos*. This peoplehood is asserted with an intense sense of outrage. In an earlier article, I analyzed this pivotal sense of outrage in Cubena's first two works. I concluded that, in the poetry:

> Black rage turned suddenly to romance, what began with a bang seemed to peter out to a whimper. However, the final soft tone is unequal to the stridency that predominates in the total work. Cubena's first novel, *Chombo*, should be going to press this year. Its tenor will determine whether the note of hope through romance sounded in the final page [of the *Pensamientos*] is really a harbinger of a new Cubena, chastened by the torment and rising above it, or whether it was the final flicker of a now definitively dead optimism.[9]

Now that *Chombo* has been published, it is clear that rage and disgust are the enduring emotions, even though there still continues to be some flicker of gentler sentiments.

Characterization is one of the primary vehicles for the expression of the author's rage. Litó's constant fury has been already discussed, but an even more artistically pertinent vehicle proves to be the non-West Indian characters of the work; types and symbols of the vicious forms of racism that have afflicted *chombos* from the very beginning of their residence in the land of exile. Indeed in the holistically transcendent framework that Cubena has established, these contemporary harriers of his people are merely the reincarnations of the original albinos whose congenital malevolence was responsible for the original evils that befell the race.

One of the contemporary manifestations of the metempsychosis of evil is Huncle Zam (a clever parody on the symbol of the U.S.A.), a Yankee overseer who had had his legs "amputated" by the avenging machete of a West Indian worker. The worker was moved to this carefully premeditated act of revolutionary violence by his intense indignation and irreparably wounded pride after Huncle Zam kicked him like an animal during the course of the normal laborer-overseer interactions in the Canal Zone work place. Huncle Zam is the namesake and kindred spirit of Sam Wallace of the short story, "El bombero" ("The Fireman"). In this story from the collection *Cuentos del negro Cubena*, Sam (Wallace), the confirmed "*revienta-negro*" (nigger killer), is also called familiarly and with brutally frank symbolism "Tío Sam" (Uncle Sam). He takes both of his sobriquets quite seriously. He is a member of a group called "The masked men of Kalifornia, Kalabama and Killinois"—the symbolism is oppressively obvious—and the proudest moment of his chosen avocation as *revienta-negro* comes after "In Mobile, Alabama ... [he] had reduced a black church to rubble" (p. 66) with a tragic toll of three young black girls.

However, the most perfect parallel of "tío Sam el revienta-negro" is, in *Chombo*, Arnulfo Simeñíquez, one of the vast clan of simian Simeñíquezes, whose sole reason for existence seems to be the expression of an insensitive and unspeakably ignorant hatred for *chombos*. The name of the clan establishes its connection with the primordial evildoers, for it refers to the characteristic deformity—*sin meñíques* (having no little fingers)—that they share with their albino ancestors. Arnulfo is a sergeant of the local police who constantly conspires to violate the civil rights of West Indians in the most brutal and direct fashion. He and his sister, Fulabuta, are officers—in fact, he is himself the president—of a grotesquely racist political organization whose benighted sociopolitical vision is adequately expressed in their slogan: "Blanquear es hacer patria" (To whiten the nation is to create a fatherland) (p. 50)—an apparent paraphrase and parody of Domingo F. Sarmiento's dictum: "poblar es civilizar" (to populate [with Europeans] is to civilize).

In my earlier article, "Big Rage and Big Romance," I had asserted that all of Cubena's characters practiced some form of deviant behavior, but, with the appearance of *Chombo* and the consequent expansion and firmer establishment of his fictional universe, it would appear that villainy is ascribed almost exclusively to non-*chombo* characters. Whereas the vast majority of the *chombos* are portrayed as normal human beings crushed by the abnormality of their environment, the non-West Indians are without exception grotesquely caricaturesque symbols of the depravity that harries the *chombos*. In every case this depravity can be reduced to some form of racism.

Cubena's style is one of going directly to the point, and so every action of these rage-expressing characters is itself a neatly formulated expression of the author's disgust. He uses the technical devices most likely to create the most intense impact with the fewest possible words: judicious use of repetition, the effective use of the punch line, of symbolism, and of "mascon" words. All of these techniques contribute to the work's *tremendismo*—a term that Adalberto Ortiz uses to characterize Cubena's style, labelling it a *tremendismo negrista*. [10] In *Chombo* this *tremendismo* is achieved principally through the process of saturation.

For example, the reader learns that on the occasion of Litó's baptism the godparents were obliged to wait in the church "because a lady was trying to seduce the parish priest after he had heard her confession" (p. 60). When Nenen and her mother obtain lowly jobs as charwomen in a brothel, we are told that they were "fired by the French madam for refusing to yield to the indecent overtures of an important North American official, her favorite client, who felt like making it with a black woman" (p. 44). These in themselves are not overwhelmingly vicious attacks. However, the plot abounds with an unrelenting series of such details. Cubena never lets up for a moment; he literally never misses an opportunity to employ the stinging detail, the little touch that contains an intense charge of anger, bitterness, and disgust. The accumulative effect of this constant barrage is staggering.

Even more staggering is his use of the most disgusting images the human mind can generate, images related to the vilest bodily functions: vomiting, urinating, and defecating. The themes of vomiting and defecation are immediately presented in the very first lines of the novel—as was seen earlier. Later on in that same paragraph, the narrator describes the sidewalk as "carpeted with the filth of stray dogs" (p. 9). The literally nauseating images will recur ad nauseam throughout the work, reaching one of the extreme limits with the description of the particular quirk that Carbón Barrescoba's depravity takes: "at the moment of orgasm, his was not the normal ejaculation, rather he would vomit all over the prostitute's face" (p. 67).

The unrelenting expression of rage would be artistically counter-productive, and Cubena attempts to achieve a balance through adroit touches of wit and some sprinkles of a kind of nostalgic lyricism. The names of the hateful non-chombo characters provide some of the most important elements of mitigating wit, as is only appropriate. Perhaps of all the many parodies the most complex and devastatingly entertaining is to be found in both the real and assumed names of Carbón Barrescoba. The fact that the coal black Carbón should be called Carbón (coal) is not particularly ingenious, but contains a certain piquant humour. However, the name he assumes for his intricately perverse adulterous relations with Fulabuta is decidedly witty in a most clever way. The name is Mierdsié Leblancú, constructed from the base "Monsieur Le Blanco," a mixture of the French title of address Monsieur and a gallicized form of the Spanish, el blanco (the white man). At this point the narrator's characteristically direct account of Carbón's perverse psychosis should be cited: "whenever Carbón Barrescoba smelled burnt cork, he would imagine that his name was Mierdsié Leblancú, who secretly longed to possess a blonde Dulcinea because under the influence of the odor of burnt cork he would find it better to have any white woman, even a whore, as long as she was white" (p. 67). Imagining himself, then, a white gentleman, no name could be more apt than Monsieur Leblanco. Cubena passes strong authorial judgement on his character's psychosis with the subtle insertion of mierda (shit) into the form Monsieur Le Blanco. The French Monsieur is often represented phonetically in Spanish literature as "mesié." With a subtly venemous twist the notion of "mierda" is added as the innocent mesié is converted into "Mierdsié." The entire name is then convincingly gallicized with the accenting of the final syllables.

The parody contained in the name of the hateful oppressor Huncle Zam is achieved by applying the special phonological rule of Jamaican Creole to the form "uncle." In contrast, for the full effect to be achieved the "z" of "Zam" has to be treated in the manner prescribed by Spanish phonology, namely, it is unvoiced except before a voiced consonant. Bartolomé de las Casas, the historic Spanish prelate whose defense of the human rights of the indigenous American people led him to the apparently unwitting and dubious distinction of being the intellectual father of the African slave trade, reappears in *Chombo* as the lecherous cleric, Bartolomé de las Chozas. The author sees the latter as a more suitable name for a variety of reasons that the reader is free to speculate on for himself, keeping in mind that "*casa*" means "house" and "*choza*" means "hut."

Relief comes too from the touches of nostalgic lyricism that punctuate the narrative. Litó is from time to time relieved of his rage by the thought of the succulent West Indian foods of his childhood prepared by Nenen, an extraordinarly good cook with a solid reputation in the *chombo* community, or by his mother. Food is one of the positive links to the essential culture of the Panamanians of Anglophone (and/or Francophone) Caribbean background, and the names of food items, as was indicated earlier, are "mascon" terms. Towards the end of the novel, during what would turnout to be his last conversation with Nenen as she lay in the hospital bed awaiting a relatively simple operation for cataracts, Litó and the old lady reminisce on the past. Naturally, Litó comes around to the subject of *chombo* food, remembering with particular fondness his trips to the market, in the company of his grandmother, "where one could buy everything still fresh." He remembers too the Sunday activity of "the grating of coconuts to provide the milk for making a succulent rice and peas" (p. 82).

The lush tropical flora and fauna are also sources of constant refreshment from Cubena's bile, stimulating the poetic spirit within him and giving free rein to his talents for the finer points of poetic expression that were so convincingly displayed in *Pensamientos*. The opening passage of Chapter Three, "Yawoada," for example, is rhapsodic in quality as Cubena has his narrator establish the setting for Litó's communion with the ancestors beneath the mango tree. It begins: "The first *quiquiriquí* of the king rooster announced very early the coming of the first light of dawn that *yawoada* (Thursday) in a backyard in the Río Abajo neighborhood. Close by the yard the happy chirping of an early-morning bird awoke the little birds in a nest hidden among the green leaves and ripe fruit of a mango tree" (p. 32). The picture that the narrator goes on to paint is one that elicits feelings of nostalgic satisfaction in any reader raised in the semirural environment of a West Indian city (I suppose the same would be true for most Third World cities): any of the inhabitants of a *Miguel Street* or a *Minty Alley*, or of the "village" in *In the Castle of My Skin*.[11]

Other West Indian Elements

After all is said and done, *tremendismo* and rage prevail in Cubena's fictional universe. We have seen that in the matter of characterization and plot *Chombo* is holistically a *chombo* novel. In fact, it is, further a "neo-African" novel. It would be simply foolish to claim that the sense of outrage is in itself peculiarly West Indian; however, the novel's pervasive sense of bitter indignation is, in fact, the most appropriate authorial response to the realities of the *chombo* human condition.

Apart from its essential structure there are other formal elements that contribute to *Chombo's* West Indian nature. Similarly, just as it was shown that the basic theme of outrage is connected to the essentially Caribbean world view espoused by the author, it can be demonstrated that there are other themes which contribute to the work's holistic and coherent expression of "West Indianness." These additional elements of structure and theme are analogous to those that have been the center of focus in the evolution of our analysis, namely: language, the themes of the plantation, of identity, of interracial love, of exile, and the voyage.

Language

Cubena's language is self-conscious in many senses. It has, in general, a quality of labored eloquence that becomes at moments truly lyrical. However, the most important aspect of his language is the quality of bold experimentation that puts *Chombo* at the very frontier of Spanish-American literary expression, and certainly too at the frontier of black writing in the Americas. This spirit of experimentation that was examined in Chapter Two is a direct result of the torturously complex linguistic situation of the *chombos*, a prototypically West Indian one. It was also seen, earlier on in the present chapter, that many of the details of Cubena's style contribute to the successful expression of the peoplehood of the *chombos* and the accompanying profoundly intense sense of outrage. The details examined were: the accumulation of stinging details— the saturation approach—the brutal starkness of descriptions, the directness of language, the ingeniously mordant wit, the general use of *tremendista* images and symbols, the basic structure of the novel in which discourse and didacticism take precedence over achieving the dramatic through the creation of a highly imaginative fictional universe that at the same time parallels and is independent of the "real" world.

Themes: The Plantation, Identity, Interracial Love, Voyage, and Exile

Cubena certainly envisages the Canal and the Canal Zone as a modern version of the plantation to which the new "slaves" come via a kind of West Indian "Middle Passage," as our interpretation in the preceding pages of this chapter has claimed. The Canal theme is, then, an extension of the plantation theme. Besides this, his treatment of the theme, from an eminently *chombo* perspective, is substantially different from that of the precursors. It is essentially a more complete picture, encompassing the latest developments in the relationship between North Americans, West Indians, and non-West Indian Panamanians over the question of the Canal. This updating illustrates further the basic precariousness of the West Indian situation in the relationship.

In the initial stages of the narrative Litó is made to confront the reality of the Canal Zone negotiations when "It was announced over radio and television that the Canal negotiations had ended in a triumph for the Isthmus." Wild scenes of national rejoicing were played out throughout the entire city. "It was carnival in August." The constant cry of the jubilant crowds was: "PANAMANIAN SOVEREIGNTY OVER THE CANAL ZONE" (p. 31). However, the pernicious element of anti-*chombo* feeling became an integral part of the celebrations, one of the choral cries echoing throughout that August carnival being, "The *gringos* are going and so are the *chombos*." The narrator explains immediately: "They were alluding to the fact that the majority of West Indian blacks managed to get a job since the North Americans gave them some opportunities on the Canal Zone" (p. 31). The cruel irony of this unfair resentment is particularly wounding to the sensitive Litó, the eldest grandson of Papa James and Nenen, and, perfectly cognizant of the long litany of horrors suffered by his grandparents, his parents, and his own generation at the hands of these so-called "benevolent" employers and protectors,

> He spent all night thinking about the insulting and unjust comments he had heard about the black folks who worked on the Canal. It seemed ironic that the descendants of those who gave sweat and blood so that the great interoceanic route could become a reality should no longer have any future in either Gatún or Gamboa. Time and time again he asked himself: "Where were the grandparents of those who now saw themselves as the owners of the Canal when my grandparents arrived from Jamaica and Barbados to pour out their sweat and blood for ten cents an hour, ten hours a day, six days a week for the ten years it took to build the Canal?" (p. 31)

In the midst of all the celebration of the final triumph of the Panamanians' just claims, Cubena's frank and direct voice of concern over the fate of the *chombos* sounds a discordant note, especially because of the tendency of the non-West Indian literary precursors as well as the present-day general public to ascribe unfairly to the *chombos* dastardly complicity with the oppressor. The note thus needed to be sounded, and Cubena, committed to the peoplehood of his people, does not shirk his perceived duty. Again and again the question of the ultimate fate of the *chombos* under the new order—post-1979—is posed, giving convincing proof of the West Indianness of the author's perspective on the Canal as plantation.

The theme of identity is consistent with the novel's basic purpose, as was seen, and Cubena's didacticism finds many ways to intensify the reader's "black consciousness." Furthermore, contrary to the incipient pattern established in his two prior works, Cubena begins, with *Chombo*, to take a serious view of African religions. An illustration of this drift towards the acceptance of religion as a powerful and positive force is provided by contrasting, for example, the dismissively stereotypic tone of "La familia" ("The Family"), from the collection *Cuentos del Negro Cubena* (pp. 85-94), with that used in the description of Litó's final visit to Nenen. On that occasion, the old lady experiencing a transcendental need for prayer turns to African religious symbols rather than the Euro-Christian ones: "When Nenen found herself alone she first of all prayed to Agayú, Yemayá, and Shango, ..." (p. 82). It is as if there has developed in Cubena a begrudging acceptance of the much vaunted anthropological tenet that African culture is religious-oriented, for the careful reader will note that his approach, in spite of the newfound respect for African religion, focuses more heavily on the elements that are less immediately perceived as strictly religious. The naming ceremony for Lito is, for example, narrated in great detail, presenting an elaborately African ritual that has all the appearances of anthropological authenticity.

It is in a similar spirit of contrived authenticity springing from an overt and militant concern with black consciousness that mention is made of the startling new facts of African history, the pre-Columbian African presence in America, for example. The very fact that Litó (Kwabena Baako Kungolo Mwinda Obadele Akinsanya) and his mother, Abena Mansa Adesimbo, have African names contributes to the essential aura of militancy. For the right to have African names is one that has to be defended through the vehicle of Nenen's reflections on the unfairness of mainstream Panama's attitudes that would unconditionally accept that the Chinese name their children born in Panama, "Wongchangchopsuiyé," and that the Italians similarly circumstanced should call their offspring "Neronguissepiespaguetti"—here again is a fine example of Cubena's mordant wit—yet take violent objection to African names: "but if the West Indian tries to preserve his Africanness, then they object with their mockery, and even accuse him of being unpatriotic, failing to recognize that it was the West Indian black who poured out most of the sweat and blood that went into the construction of the Railroad and the Canal" (p. 59). These words spoken by Nenen focus precisely on the crux of the matter, as we have pointed it out to be.

The focussing on the African past through scholarship bearing down directly on Africa rather than on the African survival elements in the traditional West Indian culture is one of the features that distinguishes Cubena from Quince Duncan. It is consistent with the self-consciousness of Cubena's style and, of course, reflects the peculiar trajectory of Cubena's intellectual development: a typically West Indian—in fact, a colonial—one in which the education process was designed principally to wean young minds away from any connection with their real African roots. Such connections were only reestablished, in some cases, in the final stages of intellectual development, and often in dramatic fashion more akin to a religious experience of conversion than to the normal evolution of point of view. While there is much of the scholarly Africanness in Duncan, there is much too of the Africannness gleaned from constant contact with the folk culture. The difference between Cubena and Duncan may ultimately be rooted in their contrasting native milieus: one urban, the other rural.

The powerful antiracist symbolism developed by Cubena is yet another facet of the theme of identity, and is certainly consonant with the tradition of rebellious black consciousness that pervades Caribbean culture, as indeed all other Afro-American cultures.[12] In *Chombo*, a most striking illustration of its use can be found in the final chapter, the mythological recapitulation of the history of the *chombos* and their most remote ancestors: "For millennia there had reigned in Nokoró a sweet peace and a black harmony until one said white day on which Kwafufo was born" (pp. 97-8). The stark directness of the style is something to which readers of Cubena will have grown quite accustomed. Into Nokoró, the mythical homeland of the African ancestors of the *chombos*, came the root of all the race's calamity, Kwafufo the albino child, "the most depraved white sheep in all of the black African fold" (p. 98). The allegory is essentially similar to the cosmogonical speculations of the Black Muslims, positing an original white devil, the source of all of humanity's evil. It is consistent with the sense of much Rastafarian thought on the matter of black-white relations. This clear reversal of the usual racist symbolism recapitulates and, in keeping with Cubena's style of repetition to the point of saturation, delivers with intense impact the final statement breaking the bonds of the black man's cultural enslavement.

Infused with the strong sense of black dignity, Cubena does not present interracial love as some rare achievement secretly longed for by the congenitally lustful black male. The serious problems it occasions are indeed not in the realm of the physical consummation of the relationship, but rather in the matter of the consequent sociological and psychological adjustment of the consenting partners. Fulabuta's sexual relationship with Carbón (already discussed) poses serious psychological problems for both, but the sexual need experienced by both parties is equally strong, and equally psychotic. In the short stories (Cuentos del Negro Cubena), a similar pattern is discernible. Dr. Cubena, of "La depravada" ("The Depraved Woman"), has a torrid yet sophisticated affair with a white woman, but she turns out to be entirely unworthy of his affections since she is a closet homosexual and a potential racist (pp. 57-64).

Presented in terms similar to those employed by Duncan and in contrast to the general pattern observed in the non-West Indian Central American authors, interracial sex is a relatively important theme in Cubena's work. In Chombo, however, the theme is not of pivotal artistic significance.

The reader will find in Cubena's work elements of the five aspects of the central journey metaphor that George Lamming sees in all Caribbean literature (see Chapter Three). The chombo community has been spawned by wave after wave of migrants from the islands, and consciousness of this fact attains almost obsessive proportions. Their collective journeys are presented as repetitions of the vicious cycle of which the slave trade was an essential element. Thus the Telémaco and the Waterloo loom large as forboding replicas of the old slave ships that plied their nefarious trade through the Middle Passage. However, the new "Middle Passage" also represents a passing to the metropolitan center, since Panama and Costa Rica became minor-league New Yorks, Londons, Amsterdams, Torontos, etc. Thus the journey of the chombos is a journey from a rural community to a basically urban setting—in the case of Panama, at least. The spiritual journey of self-realization is the major concern in the novel, and this self-realization requires a prior journey of reaffirmation back to the African roots, a journey that Litó, Nenen, as well as the narrator himself undertake with self-conscious energy and even fanfare.

As was seen earlier, an intense sense of exile haunts the consciousness of the chombos, especially those of the first generation, Papa James, Nenen, and the others. If one were to construct a dialectical model of Cubena's world view one could offer the original journey as the thesis, the sense of exile with the obsession to return as the antithesis, the synthesis being the spiritual journey of self-affirmation through the equally spiritual voyage back to the African roots. This latter dual journey of synthesis has to be entirely spiritual for the *chombos*, since their selfhood is to be attained in the physical environment of Panama. Litó and his generation are embodiments of the liberating synthesis having made something of themselves. Unfortunately Litó has had to do so in the United States, but this reality is not stressed. What is stressed is that Litó's self-fulfillment is attained in Panama, even though it is during a visit. His sister and brother are certainly made to achieve success—they become a nurse and a doctor respectively—without having to undertake any further physical journeying. The author's message on this issue is presented quite clearly through his treatment of the Panama Canal Treaty matter: the Canal belongs to the *chombos* as well, and they must have a meaningful place in the new order of things.

There is a profound and paradoxical optimism in Cubena that is at once hidden and highlighted by all the vehement outrage and disgust. His protestations, virulent as they undoubtedly are, are vital signs of a deep belief that things can be made better. Silence would have been the sign and measure of despair. The epigraph from Emerson manifests his firm belief in the power and meaningfulness of expression. The epigraph from Marcus Garvey that prefaces *Chombo* reaffirms and gives precise direction to this firmly held tenet. The ultimate proof of Cubena's optimism is his direct and explicit assertion: "Ebeyiye"—translated by the author himself as "The future will be better"— which he has emblazoned on his personal coat of arms.

Apart from the basic optimism irrefutably implied in the very structure and content of *Chombo* along with the explicitly stated faith in the future, Cubena has given additional proof of his congenital buoyancy. He has proclaimed the triumph of his own artistic vocation, announcing that *Chombo* is the first of a trilogy of novels—in fact, the manuscript of the second has already been completed. The Mexican writer, Juan José Arreola, speaking with his accustomed brilliant conciseness of expression has given the literary world one of the best metaphors for the act of writing. He sees it as a "lucha con el angel ... aquella operación metafística y muscular ... la batalla irremisiblemente perdida" (wrestling with an angel ... that metaphysical and muscular activity ... the battle that is irredeemably lost).[13] Cubena has taken the diametrically opposed view of literary activity—it may very well be that Arreola's pessimism is, in any case, more poetic than real.

The fundamental disjunction that I had formerly posited—venemous rage or intense beauty — must be revised now.[14] In fact, both the rage and the beauty continue to be present in Cubena's work, the rage equally venemous and the beauty equally intense, though not as conspicuous. The essential Cubena is an optimistic realist, fully understanding the past and present and firmly committed to ensuring the future. He is profoundly engagé in the articulating of the peoplehood of the *chombos* and in denouncing with equal vigor the assaults on that peoplehood. In so doing he has effectively affirmed his own personhood as a West Indian writer.

CHAPTER FIVE

THE NEW POETRY: ITS WEST INDIAN THEMES

With the West Indian Central Americans the development of a written poetry in Spanish seems to have lagged behind that of a corresponding prose, but the promise is exceedingly rich. This chapter will present a thematic analysis of the poetic works that have appeared to date. Such an approach will provide a critical framework for the effective appreciation of the exploding world of Central American West Indian poetry.

To date the Panamanian Cubena, the Costa Rican Eulalia Bernard, and the Nicaraguan David McField are the only Central American writers of Anglophone Caribbean origin who have published collections of their poems in Spanish: *Pensamientos del negro Cubena, Ritmohéroe,* and *En la calle de enmedio* along with *Poemas para el año del elefante* respectively.[1] Carlos E. Russell, a West Indian Panamanian who like Cubena now lives in the United States—in New York—has to his credit at least one published book of poems.[2] They are written for the most part in English and as such are outside of the purview of this present study. The Costa Rican Abel Pacheco, whose very West Indian *Más abajo de la piel* was discussed briefly in Chapter One, is not of Anglophone Caribbean origin.[3] His work, then, also lies beyond the bounds of this study.

The bulk of the material relevant to this chapter, then, is in the form of individual poems or groups of two or more published in various journals or newspapers. Gerardo Maloney, a Panamanian still living in Panama, born in 1945, stands apart from the field of "occasional" poets. So too does Carlos Rigby (born in 1945), a Nicaraguan of Anglophone Caribbean background whose poems have been anthologized principally in Ernesto Cardenal's *Poesía nicaraguense.*[4] When the prestigious Panamanian journal *Revista Nacional de Cultura* decided to dedicate an issue to the West Indians of Panama and included a small anthology of Panamanian West Indian poetry, Maloney's works constituted the majority of the poems chosen.[5] On the occasion of the Congreso Nacional del Negro Panameño (The National Conference on Black Panamanians), a national daily, *La República,* devoted a full page to the publication of Maloney's poetry, including nine previously unpublished works.[6] The other poets whose compositions appeared in the special issue of the *Revista Nacional de Cultura* were: Alberto Smith Fernández, who had two works, and Carlos Russell and Walter Smith, one work each. Cubena himself in a recent study identifies Luis Carlos Phillips, Winston Churchill James, and Urá del Drago as names to be added to the continually expanding list of active Panamanian West Indian poets.[7]

The Quest for Identity

The very structure of Cubena's book of poems bespeaks the idea of quest. The divisions present a progressive retreat (or advance) into the sphere of ideals. The present hardships of life in the land of exile engage the poet's interest in the first section, "Las Américas" (The Americas). The opening poem of this section, "In exilium," straightforwardly decries the basic state of the Central American West Indian. In the first stanza—of three—the note of sharp protest is sounded:

¡Qué desgracia!
ASHANTI soy
y me dicen
carlos (p. 8)
How unfortunate!
I am ASHANTI
and they call me
carlos

highlighting the sharp contrast between what he is and what he has been shaped into by the colonial process. The section ends symbolically with the poem "Invitación" (Invitation), a summons, echoing Regino Pedroso's famous "Hermano negro" (Black Brother), issued to elicit a more revolutionary response in his people. In "Africa," as the second section is entitled, the quest for meaning in the absurd state of exile led inexorably to the homeland and the root of his culture, but this does not satisfy the poet's soul. He finds Africa beleagured by the very same colonial forces, and all five poems of this brief section treat of the intense, unremitting struggle against the oppressor. (This will be developed in the final pages of the present chapter).

The final section of the book of rage and struggle is inconsistently, "Amor" (Love). However, a careful examination of this section will reveal that the turning to love is more than a mere retreat. Indeed, whereas the first poems unashamedly by their very titles, "Mi ninfa" (My Nymph), for example, limit the poet's interest to the most individualistic abandonment to romantic love, the succeeding ones move from the merely irrelevant specific to the relevant generic: "Negra preciosa" (Beautiful Black Woman), "Mulata linda" (Pretty Mulatto Woman), "India encantadora" (Enchanting Indian Woman). From race the poet progresses to nationality, the final seven poems having titles such as:

"Mi cubana" (My Cuban Woman), "Mi jamaiquina" (My Jamaican Woman), etc. The Americas of the first section have passed through the forge of the poetic imagination and have emerged transformed from hateful plantation into romantic paradise. Perhaps the metamorphosis is unrealistically optimistic, but optimism is the prerogative of the poet, and is literally the hallmark of this particular one. Most importantly, the metamorphosis was itself achieved through the poetic process, and this process corresponds to and reflects Cubena's archetypal quest for identity.

The identity that Cubena seeks is positive and dynamic. The quest is no self-questioning agony. It is rather an assertive affirmation of his own selfhood and that of his people. This affirmation was seen to be the principal message in *Chombo* where, as in the *Pensamientos*, it is accompanied by an appropriate denunciation of the assaults on West Indians. The title of the poem "Cabanga Africana," for example, would suggest the maudlin nostalgia for a definitively dead and now irrelevant past that sometimes passes itself off as black poetry, for *cabanga* is translated in Cubena's footnote as "nostalgia." The poem turns out to be anything but passively saccharine. It is characteristically brief, constituted entirely by the following stanza:

Me arrebataste de mi
QUERIDA AFRICA
con un diluvio de latigazos
por un puñado de monedas
y ahora una extraña cultura
es mi triste realidad.
Miserable culpable
un abrazo de muerte
es lo que anhelo darte.   (p. 11)
You snatched me away from my
BELOVED AFRICA
with a deluge of lashes
for a fistful of coins
and now a strange culture
is my sad reality.
You wretched criminal
an embrace of death
is what I long to give you.

The violent explosion of the punch line is typical of Cubena. His sense of belonging is quite firm, he knows himself to be an African cast adrift in the Americas. Even at moments when he appears to deny his blackness, as in "Mi raza" (My Race) with its,

Yo no soy negro
ni blanco
ni amarillo.

¿Mi raza?
HUMANA (p. 15)
I am not black
nor white
nor yellow.
My race?
HUMAN

what he is really affirming is his equality to any man. Seen in this light and recalling that the typical black self-denial syndrome is complemented by a desire to be white (notably absent here), his sentiment is positive and self-affirming. And indeed it is accompanied by the Cubena sense of outrage poured into the one word "malditas" (damned) that occurs in the first and last lines of the next stanza,

Malditas fronteras
panameño no soy
¿hispanoamericano?
tampoco
ni norteamericano ni ...
malditas fronteras. (p. 15)
Damned borders
Panamanian I'm not
Spanish American?
neither
nor North American nor ...
damned borders.

Again the poem is quite simple and brief, constituted by the stanza quoted above encased between the repeated verse that was cited earlier.

For Maloney as for Cubena *chombo* identity is conceived of in militant terms, there being no room for self-effacing doubt. Maloney, on one occasion when I mistakenly attributed a "¿Quien soy?" poem to his authorship, protested with vigorous pride that such sentiments had no place in his works: he knew exactly who he was. The quest for identity, then, in both of these young Panamanian writers is a campaign to firmly establish the *chombo's* basic self-worth and the value of his contribution to Panama and to humanity in general. In the terms used by Melva Lowe Ocran, another young Panamanian West Indian intellectual, they seek to ensure that *chombos* and other black Panamanians will no longer continue to be "invisible in any representation of the typical Panamanian person."[8] The idea of invisibility immediately recalls Ralph Ellison's formulation of the same problem.

The theme of identity is explored in the four Maloney poems that appear in the *Revista Nacional de Cultura* issue, but the most characteristic poetic statement on the question is contained in the final stanza of "Elaborando nuestros nombres" (Developing Our Names), a poem that by its very title bespeaks the strength and pride of self-affirmation—a poem that will be analyzed in some detail later on:

> Basta de hacer tan solo de tu existencia
> repeticiones de frases impresas de antemano sobre tu tumba
> observa bien; no has heredado un nombre
> despierta y fórjalo en hombre. (p. 103)

> Enough of this making your existence a mere
> repetition of cliches written in anticipation on your tomb
> look well; you haven't inherited a name
> wake up and make one like a man

A definite agenda is proposed for *chombos*, whose cultural heritage has been viciously and systematically assailed to the point of their being generally viewed as a people devoid of any cultural heritage, a people who have not inherited any name. The poet unconditionally exhorts his people to redress this wrong, to make manifest to the world their rich cultural heritage, thereby forging themselves into men. Maloney's tone in the stanza quoted is echoed in the last stanzas of three of his four poems.

In his prologue to Eulalia Bernard's *Ritmohéroe*, Quince Duncan ascribes to her work a primary testimonial function: "This is the basic value of Eulalia Bernard's poetry. It documents" (p. 14). The need to document is itself a function of her keen sense of identity, a sense that she proclaims in the very dedication page of her work:

> A mis ancestros y sus
> descendientes que han
> contribuido a *forjar*
> con amor nuestra *patria* (p. 21, emphasis added)
> To my ancestors and their
> descendants who have
> contributed to the *forging*
> of our beloved *fatherland*

This is a very confident statement of belonging and will contrast both with Bernard's later poetic statements in which the confidence of belonging to the new *patria* is more a desired goal than an achieved one, as well as with the general tenor of Maloney's and Cubena's sentiments on the issue. Her poem, "Esencia antillana" focuses on the process of forging the fatherland. Each of its three stanzas contains an admonition for the Costa Rican West Indian. The final one is:

> !No! Antillano.
> Necio eres si enterrar
> Tu etnia prefieres,
> que tus ojos, tu pelo, tú,
> en esencia, eres
> Antillano. (p. 50)

No! West Indian.
You are foolish if you prefer
to bury your ethnicity,
your eyes, your hair, you,
in essence, are
West Indians.

Bernard's aggressive didacticism finds an adequate outlet in the poetic form. The "!No! Antillano" with which all the stanzas begin conveys the sense of urgency, expressing the tone of warning that the poet, like the prophets of old, adopts as she attempts to steer her people along the true path to authentic, self-fulfilling identity. To make the point even more forcefully, the poet has adroitly framed the stanza between the repeated "Antillano."

The book ends on a similar note of energetic encouragement to her West Indian Central American people. The final poem is entitled significantly "Nosotros" and presents at first a rather pessimistic definition of the West Indian differential factor that can be summed up in the final lines of the first three stanzas respectively: "Nosotros somos otros." "Nosotros somos soledad." "Nosotros somos muertos." (We are other. We are solitude. We are living dead) (p. 91). All of this is rooted in the experience of exile, in the possibility of succumbing to its perils. But the tribe will not succumb if it harkens to the poet-prophet's final words:

Forjemos nuestros dioses
Entonemos frescos cantares
Nosotros somos. (p. 92, emphasis added)

Let us forge our gods
Let us sing new songs
We exist.

The same word, "forge," from the dedication reappears in this more properly combative context. The tone and the language itself recall the final stanza from Maloney's "Elaborando nuestros nombres" that was quoted earlier.

The Sense of Exile

A deep sense of being in exile pervades the literary expressions of Caribbean people, the poetry under discussion in this chapter being no exception. The opening poems of Cubena's collection, either by their titles or by their content or both, treat this theme with especial poignancy: "In exilium," "Desarraigado" (Uprooted), "Latrocinio" (Robbery), "Cabanga africana," "Las Américas," "Africano cimarrón" (African Maroon), "Triangulispano ameri-cano" (a play on words combining "triangular"—of the Triangular Trade—with

"Hispanic-American"), and "Mi raza." Bernard's "Requiem a mi primo jamaiquino" (Requiem for my Jamaican Cousin) and "Himno a Jamaica" (Song for Jamaica) spring from a similar vein. The title of Smith Fernández's "Adiós América" (Goodbye America) certainly, in itself, strongly suggests the image of travel and exile, but the work itself consists of a series of enigmatically sketched images which defy a single simple interpretation. It is in Maloney's "Nuevos nómadas" (New Nomads) that the clear sense of the title is paralleled by an equally clear sense of the content. This is the poem, then, that most forcefully expresses the theme of exile.

The title of the work, "New Nomads," is entirely consonant with the holistic approach to Black history which posits the centrality of the process of "scatteration" in the unfolding of this history.[9] According to this approach, one of the earliest cases of dispersion occurred when the area now known as the Sahara first dried up, forcing the inhabitants of the once green and thriving land to seek refuge in other parts of the great continent. The process repeated itself throughout the entire history of African peoples and thus accounts for their dispersal over the entire universe, from New Zealand to Alaska. The more or less modern history of Africans certainly lends credence to this theory, for over the past five hundred years they, the new nomads, have been the victims of significant forced mass migrations that have resulted in drastic alterations in the demographic patterns of the Americas as well as of Europe. The most recent developments in these new nomadic activities have involved countries such as Panama and Costa Rica as well as the major cities of Western Europe and North America: New York, Toronto, Montreal, London, Amsterdam, Marseille, Paris, etc. etc. Although Panama and Costa Rica have tended to be mere way stations in the migratory moves of the present century, they have played an especially important role in the "scatteration" process for the Caribbean African, as was indicated in the Introduction. Panama in particular has become the true Caribbean melting pot, where over the past century all of the major ethnic and national fragments of the Caribbean have come together in close, if not always harmonious, juxtaposition: Afro-Hispanic Caribbean people, being the so-called *negros coloniales;* Afro-English Caribbean people, being the vast majority of the so-called *chombos;* the Afro-French Caribbean people, who also constituted the tide of migrants over the past century.

It has become customary for the historians and other social scientists to divide Caribbean people on the basis of the various European colonizing ethnic groups, but no corresponding division is made on the basis of the various ethnic groupings of the African peoples who constitute the majority of the Caribbean population. There is perhaps good reason for this in that the common exposure to the traumatic and constant barbarism inflicted by the European colonizers forced the several African ethnic groups: the Ashanti, the Mandingo peoples, the Yoruba, the Congo people, the Fanti, etc. etc., towards a monolithic cultural development. The foundation for this development lay in the basic cultural similarities shared by the African ethnic groups, a consequence of many millennia of civilized existence on the mother continent. However, contemporary scholars are becoming increasingly sensitive to the differences between Caribbean Africans, and Cubena more than any other of the poets echoes this new sensitivity in his work. (We have already seen some of this in the previous chapter; more will be seen of it in the course of this present chapter). Such then is the extremely rich human treasure that Panama holds within its borders, redolent of cultural wealth that the new West Indians have only just begun to explore.

Maloney, consistent with the prevailing tradition, begins his considerations of the scatteration process with the most generally known aspect: that of the Atlantic slave trade. The poem begins with the proclamation that

En el pasado
engañados nuestros antepasados
nos vieron encarcelar y marcar
frente a un enorme espejo. (p. 98)

In the past
our deceived ancestors
saw us caged and branded
before an enormous mirror.

This bold poetic statement about the enormous indignity of slavery is placed in the context of the historical process with the repeated references to chronology: "In the past," "ancestors," and "before an enormous mirror"—the mirror being a symbol for time. The verse is free without any regular rhythm nor rhyme, but it flows with an eloquent grace.

It is with the first two lines of the third stanza of his "New Nomads" that Maloney most fully captures the sense of exile:

Mientras, nuestras tumbas sin huellas
en cualquier lugar del viento. (p. 98)
In the meantime, our unmarked tombs
all scattered to the winds.

Respect for the ancestor is the cardinal principle of African ethical and religious systems, and proper burial procedure is an integral part of this respect. So the image of the unmarked and hence unremembered graves strewn haphazardly around like objects scattered by the fickle wind is one that is particularly disturbing to anyone steeped in African or neo-African culture. However, it is an image that accurately paints the reality of the African's exile in the New World, summing up the essential experience of the new nomads. Somewhat analogous images are created by Cuebna and Carlos E. Russell. The latter, for example, in "Silenciosamente," one of the poems appearing in the special issue of the *Revista Nacional de Cultura*, evokes it powerfully with this one line: "Nosotros ...expatriados" (We...expatriated) (p. 110). Cubena, in his *Pensamientos del negro Cubena*, time after time uses such language as, "arrebataste" (you snatched) and "arrancados" (uprooted) as in the verse,

Mis antepasados arrancados
del Africa negra   (p. 11)
My forebears uprooted
from black Africa

of the poem "Africano cimarrón." Maloney's image is much more forceful and echoes the feelings articulated both poetically and in scholarly forums by Edward Brathwaite on the primordial necessity for those who have survived the Middle Passage to bury their dead. (The idea was discussed in reference to *Chombo).*

The conditions in the New World help to make the African a perpetual exile. His first condition, according to the conception presented by the poet, is that of a slave, and even the termination of his official servitude does not really ease his exile. Liberty for the African in the Americas, claims the poet, is simply "La libertad de permanecer a la deriva" (The freedom to remain adrift) (p. 98). He remains metaphorically and in many ways literally a nomad. He stands apart from the mainstream of history in the lands to which the process of "scatteration" has brought him, creating an alternative marginal culture, which, true to the guiding principle of his original culture, is religious in orientation:

Y creamos nuestros propios altares
donde el mar fuera visible (p. 98)

And we created our own altars
where the sea could be seen

The remaining lines of that stanza evoke the details of life in exile:

—Esperanzas de regresar algún día—
y volvieron a circular los secretos ancestrales
y las voces en ritmos profundos, graves,
conteniendo las plegarias y las esperanzas
llenaron los días de intenso trabajo.

—Hopes of returning some day—
and the ancestral secrets began to circulate again
and voices in profound rhythms, grave rhythms
containing the prayers and hopes
filled the days of intense labor.

The place of exile is a land of work—a plantation (as will be developed later)—and the uprooted Africans are sustained in their suffering by their ancestral culture as well as by the strong hopes of returning.

Further evidence of the transplanted African's marginality in the New World comes on the second page of Maloney's poem. Moving from the general to the particular, the poet focusses first on the entire American situation, baldly stating:

> Después vino la guerra
> poco supimos del motivo de tanta ira   (p. 99)

> Afterwards the war came
> little did we know of the reason for so much rage

As the succeeding lines will clarify, this is a reference to the wars of independence that were so crucial to the formation of the Americas as they exist today. They had little meaning for the millions of black folks who then lived in the Americas and for whom this new land had become their only home. The rest of that stanza paints a vigorously complete image of the pomp, splendor, and patriotism that were generated by and were, as well, generative of the wars: the proclamations of independence, the creation of national heroes, and all of the trappings of the foundation of nationhood. The last line deftly captures one basic aspect of this activity with the simple words, "and they began to speak of the *patria*." The persona evoked in Bernard's "Requiem a mi primo jamaiquino" is also tragically denied of a *patria* "since he never managed to get his identity card" (p. 36).

With telling irony the very next stanza in three brief lines juxtaposes the image of what all this pomp and circumstance really meant for the black "citizens" of the new *patrias*, namely:

> El trabajo se hizo más duro
> porque aparecieron los nuevos dueños
> con sus castigos y reglamentaciones. (p. 99)

> Work became harder
> because new owners appeared
> with their punishments and regulations.

This short stanza serves as the poet's introduction to the final phase of his work in which he will narrow his focus to the situation in Panama. The period of heady patriotism and foundation of nationhood for that area roughly extended over the final three quarters of the nineteenth century into the very first half of the first decade of the twentieth. Generally speaking this period was framed by two historical events of similar characteristics: the construction of the transisthmian railroad and of the Panama Canal. The poet presents in the final stanza, one that occupies one and one-half pages, the key images that accurately portray the essential features of this period.

> Y llegaron del mar los nuevos amos,
> con maletas llenas de oro
> y aprendimos a llamarlos "mister"   (p. 99)

> And new masters came from the sea
> with trunks full of gold
> and we learned to call them "mister"

says the poet simply, conveying the complex of sentiments that constitute

Panama's reaction to the events of the 1850's. The transisthmian railroad, constructed primarily to effect the reasonable transporting of the newly discovered gold from California to the East Coast, signaled the first large-scale intervention by the Anglophone United States and hearalded the future onslaught on Hispanicity by the new masters, the "misters."

One of the most important by-products of this intervention is brought to the fore with the lines

> Fuimos reclutados nuevamente
> desembarcados en nuevas tierras   (p. 99)

> We were recruited again
> set ashore on new lands.

At this point the definitive wave of *chombo* immigrants makes its entrance, and the history of the *negros coloniales* merges with that of the *negros antillanos*, conjoining two phases of the "scatteration" process. However, the struggle to belong will be a long one, and the poet must now focus on the reality of the latest arrivals' daily existence in Panama, cataloging all the particular pains of that particular plantation existence on the Canal Zone. He has thereby integrated the plantation theme into the structure of the poem. Its introduction at this point of the poem's evolution illustrates impressively its close relationship to the themes of exile and identity.

Having, then, introduced the plantation theme, Maloney goes on to elaborate it by evoking the much spoken of "green hell": the savagely intense work in the tropical forests with constant danger and discomfort. Severely handicapped by the many hostile forces at work in this green hell, the new labor force with ingenious resourcefulness succeeded in both of its monumental tasks, as the poet proclaims: "y trabajamos duro, para abrir el camino de acero" (and we worked hard to open the path of steel) (p. 99) and, then, one line later on, "y muchos vimos como se encontraron en un punto los dos oceanos" (and many of us saw how the two oceans came together at a single point). With very succinct symbolism the poet has riveted the readers emotional and intellectual interest on the transisthmian railroad and the Panama Canal. The image evoking the Canal is particularly poetic, describing with complete accuracy and force the reality of the Canal: the bridge between two oceans, the conduit through which is accomplished the miracle of their convergence.

Once the task was completed the *chombo* labor force was kept on to service the needs of the new plantation. The poet complains that "Terminada la faena nuevamente nos enviaron a la deriva" (The task being finished they cast us adrift again) (p. 99). Having no control over their destiny the *chombos* are merely shunted about at the behest of the dominant group, the notorious "misters." Thus the image consonant with the major theme of the poem, exile and rootlessness, is used to describe their new state. Theirs continues to be a purposeless existence in terms of their own needs and values; they have been sent to wander aimlessly.

One of the basic features of the West Indians' residence in Panama were the wooden tenement buildings constructed as functional living quarters for them, a modern version of the slave barracks and slave shacks. Some of these structures still exist today, and they certainly have indelibly marked the consciousness of the Afro-Antillean people. This is precisely what the poet sees when he says:

> y nos arremolinamos en cuartos pequeños de madera
> rondando el reino del fantasma
> esperando ansioso su llamada
> pero escuchamos la dureza de su voz
>
> "Only White" —
> — Gold Roll — Silver Linne [sic]
> imponiendo color a todas las cosas
> color al enfermo, color a los rezos, color a la risa,
> a la madre, a los hijos, al mundo. (p. 99)
>
> and they shunted us into small wooden rooms
> haunting the kingdom of ghosts
> anxiously awaiting their call
> but hearing only the harshness of their voice
> "Only White"
> — Gold Roll — Silver Linne
> imposing the color line on everything
> the color line on sickness, on prayers, on laughter
> on mothers, on children, on the world.

As far as each individual West Indian was concerned, his existence was framed physically, and indeed to a large extent culturally and in every other way, by the four walls of his small room in the wooden tenement building. This is the kind of room so correctly described in Beleño's pivotal scene based on Christi's death (see Chapter One). Again, the poet focusses on the raison d'être of the chombo's existence, the need to provide a pool of cheap labor.And again, this concept and the accompanying strong emotion are fully expressed with the image "haunting the kingdom of ghosts / anxiously awaiting their call." This is Maloney's way of evoking the "Central Labor Office" and all that it stands for.[10] With his image Maloney gets to the root of the entire drama of this aspect of the chombo's human condition: his desperate quest for work and the corresponding utter dependence on the "nuevos amos" who run the new version of the old plantation. And then, finally, the poet presents a series of images that completely capture the reality of the apartheid system, one of the twin cornerstones of the plantation in any and all of its various forms. To do this more effectively he uses the very terms coined by the new masters, and in their very language: "Only White" — / — Gold Roll — Silver Linne." The Manichean (to use Frantz Fanon's terminology) division and separation were unspeakably and unnaturally rigid and systematic, existing in hospitals—"color al enfermo," in churches— "color a los rezos," in all forms of entertainment—"color a la risa." The color line even entered the home, violating the individual's life in its most intimate and traditionally inviolate aspects: the relationship between mother and child—"a la madre," the relationship between siblings—"a los hijos." It affects the entire universe in which West Indian Panamanians operate—"al mundo."

This new system imposed itself "a cada uno de nuestros pasos ...·" (on every one of our steps). The poem, with the line just cited, moves into its final phase in which the metaphor built on "pasos" is central. This concluding movement of the poem consists of twelve consecutive lines, each beginning with the word "pasos," which considerably intensifies the nomadic metaphor. The poet maintains at the same time the basic universality of his perspective with such lines as: "pasos de una vida dócil y subterránea" (steps of a docile and subterranean life), or, "pasos que niegan la condición de hombre" (steps that negate the human condition). However, the last of the *pasos* returns to the specific focus: "pasos de 'chombo' aquí y en la gran ciudad" (steps taken by "chombos" here and in the big city) (p. 100).[11] Important and overwhelming as is the reality of the plantation, its effects are not as inexorable as they appear to be. The poem ends with a dramatic reversal, a flash of optimism that previews the final victory wrought through commitment to struggle. All of this is articulated in the poetic pronouncement that:

> Hoy sentimos un ritmo nuevo,
> vigor que confunde los pasos cansados, los pasos perdidos
> con las conciencias decididas. (p. 100)

> Today we sense a new rhythm
> a vigor that confounds those tired steps, those lost steps
> with committed consciences.

These three lines are the absolutely final ones of the long poem. The new nomads, while painfully aware of the bitter details of their situation, have resolved to take the steps that will firmly lead them out of their exile. Significantly, there is an unwavering and profound identification between the poet/persona and the *chombos*, symbolized in the unremitting use of the first person plural from the very beginning to the very end of the long poem.

The Plantation

Although the concern in "Las Américas" (the first section of Cubena's *Pensamientos*) is with the plight of the transplanted Africans on the entire continent, Cubena, consistent with the rest of his works, vehemently expresses his sentiments on the question of the Canal and the condition of the *chombos* vis-a-vis that reality. The extremely brief poem "Gatun," with its clever layout on the page, utters the poet's most forceful feelings on the issue, as follows:

	K	K	K
No queremos	o	o	r
	c	l	i
	a	a	n
			g
			a

ni hamburger
ni imperialista $
Teddy ladrón
queremos JUSTICIA (p. 19)

	K	K	K
	o	o	r
We don't want	c	l	i
	a	a	n
			g
			a

nor hamburger
nor imperialist $
Teddy the thief
we want JUSTICE

The uninitiated reader is helped in grasping the full significance of this powerful poem, since Cubena explains in a footnote that Gatun is an "important lake in the Panama Canal." It is situated near the Caribbean end of the waterway, not far from the town of Colon. No reader can miss the basic sense of the material pun achieved by the clever configuration of the poem; the defintive rejection of the KKK, the Ku Klux Klan, the white terriorist group that many people instinctively associate with the most hateful aspects of American racism. The finer points of the image may need some further explanation. "Koca" is simply a form of "Coca" that the poet has taken the liberty to spell with a "K," for obvious reasons. In like fashion, the word "*gringo, a*" (adjective or noun commonly used to refer primarily to white North Americans) is with poetic license transformed into "*Kringa*" through the simple step of unvoicing the initial velar stop. This physical and mental image translated into unpoetic Spanish is: "No queremos

Coca Cola gringa" (We don't want Yankee Coca Cola). In one clever swoop Cubena has riveted our attention onto the two most essential features of the American occupation of Panama and the consequent imposition of a new plantation system, namely, a vicious systematic racism, and a pernicious laissez-faire capitalism dressed up in the disarming guise of free-trade commercialism. The thoughtful reader will immediately realize that Cubena's perception is singularly acute and quite disturbing, for the twin pillars of the slave trade and the brutal colonization of the Americas were, in fact, capitalism and racism.[12]

The remainder of the poem repeats the basic sentiment with different images. Hamburger, another significant symbol of the U.S. presence in the world and certainly in Panama, is likewise rejected. The next image calls a spade a spade and has the effect of reinforcing with added vigor the more subtly expressed sentiments of the first major image. Teddy is the familiar first name of the president under whom the colonizing rape was perpetrated. He represents the entire system; he is simply "Teddy the thief." The poem ends with a demand, made even more forceful by the capitalization of the key word.

Maloney, Bernard, and the others, who live in Central America, will, of necessity, have a somewhat different perspective on the theme of the plantation, as on the matter of identity and on exile, than Cubena. There is a level of detachment and sarcasm in Cubena that contrasts with their greater attention to the practical details of accomodating to the inescapable reality. Bernard's "Educación de adultos" (Adult Education) and "Hombre tierra" (Man of the Land) clearly assume the permanence of the West Indian's presence in Costa Rica and the absolutely total commitment to his new *patria*. Both of Bernard's poems evoke role-model images of strong, independent small farmers whose existence would militate significantly against the plantation system. "Hombre tierra" begins: "Oye!. . .Hombre, Tierra!. . ./ independízate;" (Hey! Man of the Land! / be independent) (p. 89). It ends: "apuñe la tierra en tu mano fuerte / y serás el último y el primero." (grab the land in your strong hand / and you will be the last and the first.) (p. 90). The two exhortations reinforce each other and appropriately frame the entire poem, clearly indicating its sense.

Maloney's feelings about the plantation theme are manifested both directly and indirectly in "New Nomads"; and it appears that for him the plantation is the other side of the coin of exile. He subscribes to the basic premise of the plantation model, namely, that West Indians were brought to Panama to work. For Smith Fernández as well it is work that defines the essence of the *chombo's* situation in Panama; he consequently ends the poem "¿Quién soy?"—published in the issue of the *Revista Nacional de Cultura* already referred to—by defining himself essentially as a working zombie, declaring:

> Soy la sombra del Trabajo!
> Me oiste?
> De América, soy la sombra del trabajo! (p. 107)

> I am the shade of Work
> Did you hear me?
> In America, I am the shade of work!

It is most interesting that the Haitian poet and social thinker, René Depestre, should use the same image, "*zombificación*" ("zombification"), to describe the effects of neocolonialism on his fellow citizens.[13]

Africa Seen Realistically

We have already seen that Cubena has a keen sense of his African heritage. He has specific knowledge about this important aspect of his culture. Unlike so many other transplanted Africans he can, for example, differentiate between the various ethnic groups that compose the vast population of the continent of his ancestors. This was made evident in "In exilium" or in "Africano cimarrón."

This sense of reality is given special expression in the section, "Africa." The poet sees quite plainly that the trials and tribulations of the Americas are shared by his brothers and sisters on the "home" continent. He explicitly rejects any of the escapist idealism to which many have been prey. He does so boldly and forcefully in the very first poem of the section, "Chimurenga." In a footnote it is explained that the title is a word taken from Shona, a Bantu language spoken in Rhodesia (sic). The word has been translated by Cubena as WAR OF LIBERATION (his capitalization). The poem is tellingly simple; it begins:

Afrika
ayer

GHANA
   MALI
      SONGAY

paraíso de mis nanas

Afrika
hoy

   Rhodesia
   Namibia
   Sudáfrica

Afrika
yesterday

GHANA
   MALI
      SONGHAI

a paradise for my nen-nens

Afrika
today

   Rhodesia
   Namibia
   South Africa

a hell for my cousins

infierno de mis primos (p. 32)

Ghana, Mali, and Songhai, three of Africa's many great empires, are used as symbols of past glories because they are the ones that have most affected the consciousness of contemporary black people. Cubena also is acutely aware of the research uncovered by Ivan Van Sertima which points to the fact that mariners from Mali came and went between the West Coast of Africa and what is now Mexico at least one full century before Columbus "discovered" America.[14] Cubena is never content to simply sing the lost past and lament the present sorrow; his vision is always dynamically positive. In this poem, as is indeed typical, the structure is equal to the basic vision, for the poem moves from the basic complaint to the vigorous appeal for corrective action and, finally, to the successful resolution artistically articulated in the last stanza:

> Afrika
> manaña
> ZIMBABWE
>   NAMIBIA
>   AZANIA (p. 33)

> Afrika
> tomorrow
> ZIMBABWE
>   NAMIBIA
>   AZANIA

The downtrodden Rhodesia, Namibia, and South Africa have been metamorphosed—through the alchemy of poetry that will hopefully also be effective in the real world—into ZIMBABWE, NAMIBIA, and AZANIA. The use of upper case is an essential part of the symbolism as form blends with content. Such, then, is the Africa of "manana," an Africa that is profoundly linked by the very structure of the poem to the Africa of "ayer," the glorious Africa. The link is as organic as the link between yesterday and tomorrow when the today can generate from within itself the necessary forces for achieving the connection. These necessary forces are vividly evoked in the central stanza of the poem:

> Que se derrame en el Limpopo
> la sangre de los Ian Smith.
> A los John Vorster
> que la muerte les dé
> un fuerte abrazo en los Sowetos.

> Let the blood of Ian Smith
> and his breed flow in the Limpopo.
> And may death deliver a strong
> embrace to John Vorster and
> his breed in all the Sowetos.

This poem sets the tone that is maintained faithfully throughout the section as Cubena, a poetic activist, employs his art to stab at the odious oppressors.

The finest example of the offensive intensity of Cubena's poetic arms is perhaps provided by the poem "Demencia" (Madness). To be properly appreciated this work has to be quoted in its entirety, as follows:

¿Qué es demencia?
Un ratoncito portugués
que en su fantasía
se adueña de

TRES
  ELEFANTES
    AFRICANOS

¿Y qué es super demencia?
La dimunita Portugal
que se adueña de

  GUINEA-BISSAU
    MOZAMBIQUE
      ANGOLA (p. 36)

What is madness?
A little Portuguese mouse
that in its fantasy
takes control of

THREE
  AFRICAN
    ELEPHANTS

And what is super madness?
Puny Portugal
Taking control of

  GUINEA-BISSAU
    MOZAMBIQUE
      ANGOLA

The Portuguese colonial adventure in Africa is reduced to its absurd proportions with Cubena's biting sarcasm. Seen in these terms the anticolonial war becomes not only eminently reasonable, but, most of all, eminently winnable. Cubena, then, in his poetry and, as we saw earlier, in his prose attains a level of Africa consciousness that far outstrips that of any of the other poets studied in our present volume.

The Question of Names

The circumstances of their transplantation into the Americas have led many "neo-Africans" to an abiding concern over the question of their name. Malcolm X, Muhammad Ali, etc. represent some of the more publicized aspects of this kind of concern. The poets have also manifested the same concern. Nicolás Guillén, for example, in "El apellido" (My Last Name) whimsically speculates on the fate that caused him to be precisely Nicolás Guillén and not "Nicolás Yelofe, perhaps? / Or Nicolás Bakongo?"[15] Through the instrumentality of his character Henri Christophe, Aimé Césaire asks with heart rending poignancy: "Can you sense a man's hurt at not knowing the name he's called by, or to what his name calls him?" He then makes the solemn declaration in immediate answer to his question: "Only our mother Africa knows."[16] The theme is particularly relevant for the young Central Americans of Anglophone Caribbean background in view of the special circumstances of their linguistic situation—already discussed in Chapter Two.

In his pivotal "In exilium," Cubena equates his namelessness to his rootlessness. It is progressively a misfortune, an insult, and an infamy that he an ASHANTI, a CONGO, and a YORUBA should be called carlos guillermo wilson. The nontraditional entirely upper case for the African ethnic designations contrasts with equally nonstandard entirely lower case for his "slave" name, and the contrasting juxtaposition makes the point most eloquently. The strong sense of protest exuded by this poem, an echo of Césaire's complaint, has been heeded by Cubena. Following exactly the injunction issued by Maloney, Cubena has in fact "elaborated" his own name; he observed well that the name he inherited was a hollow one, and, awakening from his zombie-like trance, he has forged his own name, like a true man: Cubena. He has gone even further and forged not only a more appropriate name but an entire coat of arms which he displays and explicates in a prominent place at the beginning of each of his books.

Maloney in his poem "Testimonios" simply constructs a scenario in which the two most important—for him—cultures that compose the Panamanian "melting pot" are evoked and juxtaposed. The evocation is realized on the basis of names, for the poem consists essentially of an enumeration of the names and the characteristic qualities of certain representative figures from each of the culture groups, namely, the Afro-Antillean minority and the dominant latino white/mestizo/mulatto mainstream. For example, on the Afro-Antillean side there is Grace, who "Tuvo el primero de los siete a / la edad de trece" (Had the first of her seven / at the age of thirteen), or Bump, who "Pese a todo, ha trabajado toda / su vida" (In spite of everything, has worked / all his life) (p. 104). Bump, it must be pointed out, is one of those ingenious nicknames for a true-life character, quite well-known in Panama City. He has the physical handicap of a humpback but, in spite of this, makes a living washing cars—his picture appears on one of the back pages of the issue of the Revista Nacional de Cultura to which we have been referring, along with the pictures of other West Indians and West Indian scenes. "Y del otro lado" (And on the other hand) (p. 105), the other side is represented by, for example, "El Señor Ministro de / Estado José Angel Guardia —" (Mr. Minister of / State Jose Angel Guardia —), or by "Doña

Aurora — Escritora" (Doña Aurora — A writer), or by "Alfredo — Diputado e ingeniero" (Alfredo — A congressman and engineer) (p. 105).

Eulalia Bernard's "Directorio telefónico" (Telephone Directory) raises the question in an apparently playful way, focussing on the non-Hispanic nature of the names of many "pure" Costa Ricans, those of the ruling class: the "...insky's," the "...man's," etc. Beyond the levity there is in the poem a very indirectly expressed demonstration of the falacious base of the unstated principle that non-Hispanic names are badges of inferiority.

The concern with the question of names is related to both the matter of language and the quest for identity. The present state of development of Afro-Antillean poetry from Central America does not permit a lengthy analysis of the theme; however, it is one that promises to be of some significance in the future development of this new poetry.

Interracial Love

In Cubena's *Pensamientos* love is presented dramatically as the solution as "despairing range [turns] to hopeful romance"[17] true to the romantic tradition. In spite of the apparent inconsistency there is a certain organic wholeness in the development and structure of the book (as was seen earlier). There is a certain sense of American continental identity in the final love poems of Cubena's book, and this, as we pointed out earlier, is entirely consistent with the basic thrust of the work. Thus the final seven poems are entitled "Mi cubana," "Mi jamaiquina,"etc. Nationality, then, in the end transcends race. This is significant in a poet such as Cubena, in a book such as the *Pensamientos*. It obviously represents a particular choice, a definitive stance, and can be interpreted as the final victory over racism—perhaps a victory conceived of in overly idealistic terms, but idealism is the prerogative of the poet. It is quite clear that Cubena's approach to the question of interracial love and sex is again in this instance quite consistent with what we have posited to be the West Indian writer's distinctive treatment of the theme. These relationships are consummated without any serious material obstacles; furthermore, in Cubena's poetic scenario, the attendant psychological and sociological problems have also been resolved. None of the other poets has as yet addressed himself to this theme.

The central themes of the new poetry can be identified as: the quest for identity, the sense of exile, the vision of the plantation, the sense of the importance of Mother Africa as a spiritual homeland, the sense of the importance of language and the process of naming, the theme of interracial love and sex. It is clear that these themes coincide with those that have been found to be germane to our analysis of Central American West Indian prose.

Artistic excellence is normally achieved only through a harmonious balance between form and content. It would seem, then, that the new Central American West Indian poetry will not cross the threshold of excellence until, like the other poetry of the rest of the Caribbean, it undergoes an artistic revolution in its formal aspects: until the "nativizing" process deeply affects the form of the new poetry. Then perhaps there will be calypso poems, and others that closely mirror the formal structures of West Indian oral literature. In this regard Eulalia Bernard has two poems, "El carnaval" and "El carnaval en América Latina," which, while not being carnival songs or calypsoes properly so called, at least represent a beginning. The fine young critic, J. Bekunru Kubayanda, sees Carlos Rigby's "Si yo fuera mayo" as incorporating significant technical innovations, for example, "ideophonic sounds like *sim-saima-mimalo* (a creolization of the Spanish *sin desmayo,* used in reference to the faltering dance steps of a local policeman); *shiqui shaque shiqui shaque* (a rhythmic harmonization of maracas); and *maya lasique ma-yaya-o* ... / *mayaya lasiqui mayaya-ooo* ... (p. 309)."[18]

If we accept the centrality of religion in the culture of African and "neo-African" peoples, then it would be reasonable to expect that the religious theme would be the most apt catalyst in the generation of authentic Central American West Indian poetry. By the same argument it would be entirely reasonable to expect the religious influence not to be one-sided, neither exclusive to form nor to content. The argument appears to be supported by the fact that neither Cubena nor Maloney has demonstrated any special interest in the religious theme. Duncan, who has, is not as yet a published poet. The promise is, however, undoubtedly quite rich; and "the future will be better" in this area as well.

CHAPTER SIX

CONCLUSION: TOWARDS A PAN-CARIBBEAN LITERATURE

To hell
with Af-
rica
to hell
with Eu-
rope too,
just call my blue
black bloody spade
a spade and kiss
my ass. O-
kay? So
let's begin

Edward Kamau Brathwaite

The preceding pages have attempted to demonstrate that a group of Central American authors of Anglophone Caribbean origin has begun to create a literature in Spanish that is essentially similar in form and content to all other Anglophone literature emanating from the Caribbean. It needs only to be reaffirmed in this concluding chapter that this similarity is based on an essential thread of homogeneity that runs through all Caribbean cultures and hence all Caribbean literary expressions. This homogeneity is what constitutes "West Indianness" in literature: it can be viewed as a context or an intellectual framework in which literature emanating from the region can best be appreciated and explained. Our last chapter (Chapter Five), for example, created such a context—that was more than merely heuristic—to explicate the new poetry produced by West Indians in Central America.

With all due respect both to Descartes and to Cubena's *abuelita africana* we could, at this point, personify "pan-Caribbean literature" and have her/him say, "I have been explained therefore I am." The quick-witted critic might offer the rejoinder, "Yes, but only in the mind of the explainer." However, the goal of the academic exercise is ultimately the creation of notional existences in receptive minds. It would be most rewarding if the exercise we have just engaged in—both the reader and I—were to have attained at least this basic level of success: that "pan-Caribbean literature" should exist, at the very least, in the minds of the explainer and of those attending to the explanation. One final way of ensuring this existence would be to retrace the portrait of pan-Caribbean literature that has emerged in the course of our study. "O- / kay? So / let's begin."

In the final section of the Introduction, we cited the titles of books that proclaimed the pan-Caribbean approach: *Race and Colour in Caribbean Literature, Black Images;* and referred to works by Knight and Cudjoe.[1] Knight, in his introduction, presents as one of the major assumpitons "that the sum of the common experiences and understandings of the Caribbean outweight the territorial and insular differences or peculiarities. To speak therefore of Haitian, Jamaican, Cuban, or Caribbean characteristics should not be to speak of them as mutually exclusive; the first are merely variations or components of the last" (p. x). One page later, speaking in the same vein, he claims explicity:

> In my view, the region comprises one culture area in which common factors have forged a more-or-less common way of looking at life, the world, and their place in the scheme of things. All the socieities of the Caribbean share an identifiable *Weltanschauung,* despite the superficial divisions that are apparent. ... Moreover, the Caribbean peoples, with their distinctive artificial societies, common history, and common problems, seem to have more in common than the Texan and the New Yorker, or the Mayan Indian and the cosmopolite of Mexico City do in their respective nations of the United States and Mexico. (p. xi).

Almost two decades earlier, the late Professor G. R. Coulthard, in his *Race and Colour in Caribbean Literature*, had laid the foundation for pan-Caribbean literary criticism. His pan-Caribbeanness emerged more through the clear implication of the title and the struture of his work than through any clearly stated and explicated set of assertions. The closest he comes to the declaration of a pan-Caribbean literary essence is the following: "The Negro has left a deep imprint on the Caribbean way of life, not only in music, dancing, customs, food, religious beliefs and practices, language—all things which are easily verifiable as of African origin—but in something more subtle in the spirit of the place, not so much a way of life as a feeling of life" (p. 79).

It was in the 1962 appendix, "From Toussaint L'Ouverture to Fidel Castro," to his 1938 classic, *The Black Jacobins: Toussaint L'Ouverture and the San Domingo Revolution*, that C. L. R. James made the declaration that "The history of the West Indies is governed by two factors, the sugar plantation and Negro slavery."[2] This cryptic summation of the history and spirit of the region — already presented in our Introduction — is a capsular version of the declarations of Knight and Coulthard; and it is one of the most productive insights in Caribbean scholarship. It obviously is consonant with the fundamental view presented in the original work (1938). The same view of the Caribbean constitutes the basis of the late Eric Williams' *Capitalism and Slavery* or his *From Columbus to Castro*, a comprehensive history of the region in an obviously—from the very title—pan-Caribbean mode.[3] Indeed Dr. Williams authored a little-known literary study, "Four Poets of the Greater Antilles," that could be considered one of the pioneering works of pan-Caribbean literary criticism.[4]

The current researcher in addition has available to him two most important research tools which can indeed be considered the "compasses" of pan-Caribbeanness. They have been edited respectively by Donald E. Herdeck et al. and Lambros Comitas[5] — they were reviewed together in a recent essay of mine.[6] Pan-Caribbeanness in literature is, of course, evinced in many other works, critical as well as creative. Selwyn R. Cudjoe's was mentioned as one such work.

In summary, then, these various formulations all present a common Caribbean "spirit," "culture," "*Weltanschauung*," the communalities far outweighting the differences. Coulthard and James explicity, and Knight, by inference, have declared the common African heritage to be the most important source of "West Indianness." Our own introductory presentation entirely endorsed these views; in fact, our critical framework was premised on them. Our formulation, however, went one step further—to the logical conclusion— by including the rimland areas of the Caribbean sea in the concept of the Caribbean. Most importantly, we have demonstrated explicitly that a West Indian literature written in Spanish can and indeed does emanate from at least two rimland nations: Panama and Costa Rica.

There is an opposing point of view. It is sustained by a group of scholars who, even today, are impressed with the diversity of the region, seeing the uniqueness of the Caribbean as its cultural pluralism. For them the Caribbean is a fascinating mosaic of diverse cultural elements all blending into a marvelous whole, but each maintaining its respective individuality. This view would posit Africanness as but one of the many elements that make up the mosaic. Herein lies the fundamental difference from the view that I espouse, for I see Africanness as the basis of a new culture, an "identifiable *Weltanschauung*," a "spirit," that is peculiarly Caribbean. This is not to say that there have not been generated in the Caribbean cultural expressios that cannot be in any way termed "neo-African": such cultural expressions as those of the East Indians of Suriname, or Trinidad and Tobago, or Guyana, the various Amerindian cultures of the rimland nations: the Cuna in Panama, the Mayan in Guatemala, Belize, and Mexico, for example. Such cultural expressions are legitimately Caribbean, and the uniqueness of the regional experience is precisely the tolerance and warm acceptance of these rich cultures. However, they are not cosidered by any serious thinker as "mainstream" Caribbean. Whenever one thinks of a culture that one could classify unhesitatingly as Caribbean *sui generis*, one frequently conceives instinctively of some sort of neo-African cultural expression. This is precisely what Coulthard claimed, and what James's statement pithily declares, and it is the inference that we have drawn from Knight: no bond is as important and universal in the region as the bond of the common African heritage. The "Mosaic theory" that would equate the neo-African to the neo-Hindi or even the neo- or residual Mayan, etc. is simply out of step with the glaringly obvious fact that the vast majority of the population of the area as a whole is of African origin. In the poet's somewhat colorful and dramatic language, Edward Kamau Brathwaite proclaims this basic truth:

> Ninety-five per cent of my people poor
> ninety-five per cent of my people black
> ninety-five per cent of my people dead
> you have heard it all before O Leviticus O Jeremiah
> O Jean-Paul
> Sartre[7]

Over the course of the years of colonization and slavery, the African became the new native of the Caribbean area, replacing the Amerindians who were decimated by the genocidal effects of Europe's "civilizing" presence. Although the Europeans of various ethnic origins—tribes—dominated the region, they were always a minority; the masses have been for centuries the people of African origin. Even in islands like Cuba and Puerto Rico, where the masses are composed of people with considerable degrees of European ancestry, the African presence is strong. So much so that in recent times Fidel Castro could claim—obviously with a great degree of political opportunism— that Cuba and Angola were inextricably connected by ties of ideology and of *la sangre* (blood). The same claim could be made for Puerto Rico, at least in so far as the "blood" (i.e. the racial) ties go. Isabelo Zenón Cruz and Carlos More have presented documentation which, for Puerto Rico and Cuba respectively, amounts to the scholarly versions of Fidel Castro's demagogic but substantially accurate pronouncements.[8]

Since the African has been demographically dominant in the Caribbean, his culture has been correspondingly dominant. This assertion runs counter to many sacred beliefs that have passed for scientific fact. In deference to these "false theologies" (which would require an entire book to refute) it would be expedient to simply claim, if not dominance, at least a significant impact and contribution of Africa's sons and daughters to various aspects of Caribbean culture; Coulthard's formulation quoted earlier will undoubtedly be accepted by any reasonable person familiar with the region as self-evident. Of the spheres of African cultural influence listed by Coulthard, language is most important, for it is precisely on language that Europe's cultural hegemony has been traditionally premised. Basing themselves on the dictum (allegedly self-evident) that the language makes the culture, the propounders of Euro dominance have pointed with some degree of satisfaction to the indelibly fundamental impact made by European tribal differences on the languages of the Caribbean. Recent research in the field of creolistics has, however, suggested an entirely different interpretation of the linguistic situation in the Caribbean. According to this more recent view, the real "native" languages of the Caribbean are not Spanish, French, English, Dutch—European languages— but the various creoles derived partly from these. The creoles are posited to be synthetic languages formed from a tribe-specific European lexicon—Spanish, French, etc.—on the foundation of an African syntax that was not tribe specific. Hence the bases of these languages and their communality are rooted in Africa, not in Europe.[9] In Chapter Two we saw that the linguistic situation that prevails among the West Indians of Panama and Costa Rica is essentially representative of the entire region.

Creolization in language is mirrored in other cultural areas: syncretism in religion, for example, is analogous to creolization; and syncretism is indeed a most active process in Caribbean culture. We focussed on religion since it was so relevant to the discussion of Duncan's work, and also because religion, as we indicated, has been found by the majority of researchers to be central to Caribbean culture. We saw that all the Afro-folk religious forms of the Caribbean involved some degree of syncretism. We also saw that the constitutent elements were common to them all. Thus Pukumina, the folk religion from Jamaica which passed over with the migrants to Costa Rica, is derived and related to Kumina, which is itself essentially similar in beliefs, practices, and above all, in rituals to Shango, *Santería,* Voodoo, and even *Candomblé.* Furthermore, obeah was seen to have turned up not only in Costa Rica and Panama, but in Trinidad, Guyana, Jamaica—of course—among other lands. Religion, then, a unifying factor in Caribbean culture, also functions as a unifying factor in Caribbean literature.

Food, too, is part of a people's culture, and again the African influence is significant, if not dominant. Our analysis did not stress the pan-Caribbean nature of the "mascon" food items that we identified. We did, however, focus on their essential origin in and hence link with Jamaican culture. All of the food items thus identified are important in the cultures of all the other Caribbean territories, even if the nomenclature may differ slightly: bammy, black pudding, souse, patty, yam, yampi, codfish, peas and rice, breadfruit, plantain, callaloo.

Since all the socioeconomic, political, geographic, and historical experiences of the Caribbean territories have been essentially similar, the general cultural history has followed the same pattern of evolution. Specifically in written literature, one finds that a true Caribbean expression did not appear anywhere until the 20th century when the gap—the Manichean gap as Frantz Fanon terms it—between the Afro-inspired oral literature of the folk and the scribal literature of the Euro-centered elites began to be closed.[10] For the folk are the ultimate repository of any national culture, and thus the ultimate referents in the creation of a truly national literature. The gap began to be closed, for example, in the novel when the peasant became the protagonist: in *Jane's Career* (1914), for example.[11] In poetry the gap was closed generally through the wedding of oral folk forms with scribal ones: as in Nicolás Guillén's *son* poems[12] or Edward Kamau Brathwaite's calypso- and reggae-poems.[13] Of course, in both genres the use of creole languages went a long way towards bridging the gap. The 1930's was the decade in which the entire region came alive to the gap-closing process, and there sprung up the most productive movements and schools: negritude in the Francophone Caribbean, *negrismo* in the Spanish Caribbean, and the yard novel, for example, in Trinidad and Tobago. The West Indian Central American literature that we considered is of much later origin, and is consequently a legitimate hier to all this literary ferment. The themes we identified as fundamental are all related to the same literary awakening that has taken place in the entire region: identity (along with race and protest, according to Nettleford's formulation), exile, the plantation, the Middle Passage, the ancestors, Africa, religion, black dignity—particularly in the question of interracial sex—religion, and of course the entire question of language.

Central American West Indian poetry still has some way to go with regard to the closig of the gap, in both content and form. There is still no reggae poetry, nor calypso poetry. In fact, on one occasion I asked Maloney about the absence of calypso poetry in his work. He replied that he did not feel well enough versed in the calypso form to use it. We saw that Duncan—who so far has published no poetry—is by far the most West Indian of the authors studied, because of his profound knowledge of and inspiration in the folk tradition. A most important formal feature that has been West Indianized is the language of the new literature, even the poetry. In the prose we saw that plot and characterization, elements of structure, had, in general, greatly benefited from the rich contributions of West Indian folk culture.

In the course of our analyses we have presented concrete similarities between works by the Central American writers and those of their peers in the other parts of the Caribbean: Anglophone, Francophone, as well as Hispanophone. For example, we saw that Wilson Harris's *Palace of the Peacock* and Duncan's "Los mitos ancestrales" were both constructed on characters who had already died. We saw too that *La paz del pueblo*, like most of Duncan's work, had an aura of mystery and symbolism about it that reminded us also of Harris's novel (see Chapter Three). There are similarities in the structures of *Chombo* and Alejo Carpentier's *El reino de este mundo* (see note 4 of Chapter Four). These kinds of precise instances of comparison could be greatly multiplied; however, ours is not a comparativist approach. We attempted to limit ourselves to the internal evidence, examining the body of works from Central America for all the features that bespoke their "West Indian" (in both the limited and unlimited senses expounded in the Introduction) connections.

Evidently, very interesting and productive comparativist analyses could result from the groundwork laid in our book. Every element of form and content that we identified as West Indian could be examined in any work of West Indian literature from the rest of the entire Caribbean. On the theme of religion the critic could, for example, undertake a most fruitful comparative study of Michael Thelwell's *The Harder They Come* and Duncan's *La paz del pueblo* as well as his "La rebelión pocomía."[14] In the Jamaican novel the political role of Jamaican Afro-folk religion is developed in as full a manner as in Duncan's two works. In the two novels the theme is integrally conjoined to that of the black peasant's harmonious relationship to nature. An even more sweeping list of works could be found that treat the subject of obeah and obeah men and women in a manner consonant with Duncan's approach, especially in *Los cuatro espejos*. We could add to the works already mentioned in our Chapter Three the important Jamaican novels, *Brother Man* by Roger Mais and even *The Harder They Come*.[15] The question of names was presented as an important West Indian theme, although the new poetry was seen to be not extensive enough to provide as yet much material. I have, however, found that the insight presented both in Chapter Five and tangentially in Chapter One is corroborated by my reading of other Caribbean works. One, for example, finds correspondences between the naming customs—part of the overall language question—as depicted in the *Harder They Come*—the use of "Maas Nattie," and "Miss Mando," for example—and in Joseph Zobel's Martinican novel, *La rue cases-nègres* (translated by Keith Q. Warner as *Black Shack Alley*)—the use of "Mam'zelle Délice" and "M'man Tine," for example. [16]

Our book has provided a line of approach both for the critic and the general reader of West Indian literature, from Central America and elsewhere in the region. Since the output of Caribbean literature from Central America undoubtedly will increase greatly in the future, we believe that this work has been a most timely contribution. Its first test could be the poetry of the Nicaraguans, David McField and Carlos Rigby—their names accurately bespeak their Anglophone Caribbean ancestry. We indicated (see note 18 of our Chapter Five) that their work was not clearly identifiable as West Indian according to the criteria and the line of analysis that we have demarcated. Of course, this judgement could reflect unfavorably on either the line of analysis or the works so judged. It is our firm contention that the analysis is sound.

Fanon and Amilcar Carbal's Dialectical Theory of Identification readily accounts for the works of Rigby and McField.[17] It posits three phases in the evolution of a colonized artist or intellectual: capitulation, revitalization, and radicalization. The capitulation stage is one of complete assimilation of the culture of the dominant group. The revolutionary young Caribbean poets who in 1932 in Paris launched the one and only issue of Légitime Défense, hurled invective at those fellow citizens who sported a "personalité d'emprunt," taking foolish pride in the fact that a white person could read their writings and not tell that the author was black.[18] It would be in poor taste indeed, and, in fact it would be a display of poor critical judgement as well, to accuse the two Nicaraguans in the terms used by the launchers of Légitime Défense, or even in the terms of the Fanon-Cabral theory. It is clear, however, that our critical framework allows for a wide range of works. We find that those we have selected for detailed analysis are the most interesting for us. Obviously, since both Rigby and McField are Central Americans of Anglophone Caribbean ancestry, they are West Indians according to our definition; and their literature represents one kind of West Indian literature. In so far as we have made a judgement— and it is one of personal taste—we find their West Indian response to be not as interesting and aesthetically stimulating as that of the other writers we have studied. This latter response is, according to our approach, demonstrably more coherently West Indian.

The success of our line of approach will be determined ultimately by its value as a productive critical tool for assessing West Indian literature; especially that which has emanated, and, according to our findings, will continue to emanate in an ever increasing flow from Central America—literature of Spanish expression. Chapter Five demonstrated the success of the analysis with the new Panamanaian poets. We believe that we have set out on a new path that will lead to greater insight into the total phenomenon of pan-Caribbean literature and culture. The path is charted by the "compass" of "West Indianness" in literature. The end of our present discussion is really a beginning. "O- / kay? So / let's begin."

Notes

Notes

Introduction: The "Scatteration" to Central America

[1]The interisland contacts are well-documented and generally well-known. The case of the migrations of Haitians to Cuba during the epoch of the Haitian Revolution and during the first decades of the 20th century is a good example. So too is the important demographic shift initiated in the 18th century from the Francophone islands to Trinidad. In the case of the contacts between the islands and the rimlands, they are not so generally known but with regard to the present day one has only to go to Caracas, for example, to find numbers of immigrants from the Spanish, Dutch, French, and English Caribbean islands. The same situation may exist to a lesser extent in Colombia. The contacts of the past are quite evident and some of them are mentioned in the next paragraph.

[2]For more information see Douglas Mac Rae Taylor, *The Black Carib of British Honduras* (New York: Wenner-Green Foundation, 1951) and Justin Flores, *The Garifuna Story Now and Then* (California: n.p., 1979).

[3]For more information see Quince Duncan and Carlos Meléndez, *El negro en Costa Rica*, 5th ed. (San José: Editorial Costa Rica, 1978), pp. 68-82.

[4]See Duncan and Meléndez, p. 104.

[5]See Leslie B. Rout, Jr., *The African Experience in Spanish America* (London: Cambridge Univ. Press, 1976), p. 211. The most impressive documentation of this claim is to be found in an as yet unpublished paper by Winston R. Welch "Evolución de la población negroide en Panamá" (1978).

[6]See Duncan and Meléndez, especially p. 55.

[7]The reader should pay special attention to the terms *negro colonial, antillano, afro-antillano, afro-antillano panameño, crillo,* and *chombo* as they will be used frequently throughout the book. The list of names given to Central Americans of Anglophone Caribbean ancestry is quite long. It includes, besides those already mentioned, *jamaicano* or *jamaiquino* (Jamaican), *afro-caribeño* (Afro-Caribbean), and *chumeca* or *chumecaman* (terms that will be explained further later on). The latter two terms along with *chombo* are by and large considered disparaging—*chombo* being the strongest. All of the names designating "West Indians" from Central America will be used interchangeably throughout the book. *Criollo* (Creole), it should be noted, is a most imprecise term, having different and mutually exclusive referents in different regions, and sometimes in the same region. In addition, the reader should attend to a simple point of Spanish morphology which will facilitate his understanding of the use of these and other terms in this book: the "o" ending denotes usually masculine singular, the "a" feminine singular, the "s" indicates plural, the masculine singular is the form usually cited in lists.

[8]See Manuel Ramírez, III, "Recognizing and Understanding Diversity: Multiculturaism and the Chicano Movement in Psychology," in *Chicano Psychology*, ed. Joe L. Martínez, Jr. (New York: Academic Press, 1977), pp. 343-353 for the original ideas and Buena I. Dawkins-Smart, "The Conflict-Replacement and Flexibility-Synthesis Models Relative to Language Attitudes and Language Choices of a Panamanian Minority Group," M.A. Paper UCLA 1980 for further explication, particularly with regard to the situation in Panama.

120

[9]For further details on the questions of religion, education, economics and politics, see the works by the following authors cited in the Bibliography: John and Mavis Biesanz, Roy S. Bryce-Laporte, Buena I. Dawkins-Smart, Duncan and Meléndez, Melva Lowe-Ocran, and Allen G. Morton.

[10]In fact, on the basis of this "Africanity" and the common, profoundly shaping plantation experience, the concept of "Caribbean" can be extended to include even such places as Brazil, Peru, and even Louisiana.

CHAPTER ONE

Unless expressly stated to the contrary, I am responsible for all translations into English of the original French or Spanish quotes used in this book.

[1]Rodrigo Miró, *La literatura panameña* (Panamá: Serviprensa, 1976), p. 277. This opinion, in my view, aptly represents the position of those Panamanians who have steadfastly set themselves to create an image of the typical Panamanian, which defies all the demographic and cultural evidence. I have dealt with precisely this question in my article "A New Panamanian Poet's Promising Quest for Identity: The Case of Gerardo Maloney," *Plantation Society in the America*, 1 (1981), 376-386.

[2]Mélida Ruth Sepúlveda, *El tema del Canal en la novelística panameña* (Caracas: Universidad Católica, 1975), p. 70.

[3]Jorge Turner, Prólogo, *Gamboa Road Gang*, by Joaquín Beleño C. (Panamá: n.p., 1959), p. 10.

[4]*Latino* refers to those whose sole native language is Spanish, in contrast to the *criollos*, *antillanos*, *chombos* (to use just three of the interchangeable terms) for whom English Creole is also a native language. Of course, some *latinos* are black, belonging to the *negro colonial* group. The term will be used throughout in accordance with the linguistic norms set forth at the end of note #7 of the Introduction.

[5]Joaquín Beleño C., *Curundú* (Panamá: Ministerio de Educación, 1963), p. 122. All further references to this work appear in the text.

[6]*Gringo* refers to the white Anglo-Saxon type, especially the U.S. North American. Again, the rules of Spanish syntax will affect the spelling of the various forms of the term used throughout.

[7]*Luna verde* (n.p.: n.p., n.d.), p. 142.

[8]Joaquín Beleño C., *Gamboa Road Gang* (Panamá: n.p., 1959), p. 83. All further references to this work appear in the text.

[9]Beleño also wrote *Flor de banana* (1965), a novel with no reference to the West Indian presence in Panama.

[10]A reference undoubtedly to the great economic crisis that afflicted much of the Western world during the 1930's.

[11] Demetrio Aguilera Malta, *Canal Zone* (Santiago, Chile: Ercilla, 1935), p. 67. All further references to this work appear in the text.

[12]This is the title of both an article by Alvaro Sánchez M. anthologized in a work co-authored by Quince Duncan and Carlos Meléndez, *El negro en Costa Rica*, 5th ed. (San José: Editorial Costa Rica, 1978), pp. 173-189; and an entire separate work by Quince Duncan, *El negro en la literatura costarricense* (San José: Editorial Costa Rica, 1975).

[13]Carlos Luis Fallas, *Mamita Yunai*, 5th ed. (San José: Lehmann, 1977), p. 15. All further references to this work appear in the text.

[14]The law, in article 5, paragraph 3 states: "Colored people are hereby forbidden from employment in such jobs (the production and exploitation of bananas) in the Pacific zone" (quoted by Duncan and Meléndez, p. 92).

[15]Quince Duncan, *El negro en la literatura costarricense* (San José: Editorial Costa Rica, 1975), p. 14. All further references to this work appear in the text.

[16]Joaquín Gutiérrez, *Puerto Limón* (San José: Editorial Costa Rica, 1976), p. 90. All further references to this work appear in the text.

[17]Alvaro Sánchez M., "El negro en la literatura cotarricense," in *El negro en Costa Rica*, ed. Quince Duncan and Carlos Meléndez, 5th ed. (San José: Editorial Costa Rica, 1978), p. 187. This

work is mostly authored by Duncan and Meléndez. Thus, the few pieces by other authors that have been included can be considered to reflect rather closely the opinions of the authors/editors.

[18]*El jaspe* (San José: "Repertorio Americano," 1956). *Historias de Tata Mundo* (San Jose: Editorial Costa Rica, 1966).

[19]*La cattleya negra* (San Jose: Editorial Costa Rica, 1967), p. 36.

[20]This paradigm is offered only as a heuristic device for analyzing the majority of the literature under discussion. It is not proposed as a scientifically accurate tool for general historical and sociological analysis. For the situation has become too fluid what with the Carter-Torrijos Treaty returning the Canal to Panamanian sovereignty in 1979, for example, and the gradual loss of influence of the United Fruit Company in both Costa Rica and Panama over the years.

[21]Whereas Abel Pacheco can be considered "Caribbean" or "West Indian" in the broadest sense of the terms that was elaborated in our Introduction, he does not belong to the group of Central Americans of Anglophone Caribbean background. Consequently, for the sake of clarity and consistency he has to be separated for the purposes of our analysis from those West Indians living in Central America who do have an Anglophone Caribbean background.

[22]*Más abajo de la piel* (San José: Editorial Costa Rica, 1972), p. 11.

[23]See in particular "Concerning Violence" in *The Wretched of the Earth*, trans. Constance Farrington (Suffolk: Penguin, 1967), pp. 27-84.

[24]*Mestizaje* is the term used to describe the process of racial blending that has occurred in Latin America over the years.

[25]This is one of the prime postulates of Professor Stanley Cyrus, one of the outstanding critics in the field of Afro-Hispanic literature.

[26]These short stories appear in the collection *Cuentos del negro Cubena* (Guatemala: Landívar, 1977).

[27]For more on this idea see Ian I. Smart, "The African Heritage in Spanish Caribbean Literature," *The Western Journal of Black Studies*, 5 (1981), 23-31.

CHAPTER TWO

[1]The concern with language is a perennial one in West Indian literature, as it is with all literatures of colonized peoples. In the Caribbean, it could be claimed that the various creoles, struggling now for acceptability and legitimacy, constitute embryonic national languages. The problem of language is, of course, compounded in the case of the West Indians from Central America. Their situation, in fact, parallels that of such groups as, for example, the Chicanos in the United States. For more on the question of creoles see Mervyn Alleyne, *Comparative Afro-American* (Ann Arbor: Karoma, 1980).

[2]*El tema del Canal en la novelística panameña* (Caracas: Universidad Católica, 1975), p. 67.

[3]Joaquín Beleño C., *Curundú* (Panamá: Ministerio de Educación, 1963), p. 135. All further references to this work appear in the text.

[4]The speech can only be fully appreciated in the original language. However, it could be freely translated into a creolized conversational Trinidadian English as follows: "Liequí boy, this is how the business is, partner.... Is like this! If you get tough, you go find your mother and father in the street. And that child! You well know that we don't like to play round here ... and whips waps we gone by another woman who like the business. You see what I talking about ...?"

[5]Joaquín Beleño C., *Luna verde* (n.p.: n.p., n.d.), p. 50. All further references to this work appear in the text.

[6]F. G. Cassidy and R. B. Le Page are silent on this matter in their *Dictionary of Jamaican English*, 2nd ed. (London: Cambridge Univ. Press, 1980), but the word seems most likely to have been derived from the expression "sparring partner."

[7]Michael Thelwell, *The Harder They Come* (New York: Grove, 1980), has opted for the spelling *bwai*, which he claims is the most effective and accurate.

[8]This certainly contradicts the information I have received from my Panamanian friends. It also seems quite strange in view of the fact that the forms "gal" and "galcita" (derived from "girl") exist.

[9]The list of such works would include the following Spanish American classics: Alonso Carrió

de la Vandera's *El lazarillo de ciegos caminantes* (1773), Jorge Isaacs' *María* (1867), José Hernández' *Martín Fierro* (1872), and José Eustacio Rivera's *La vorágine* (1924)—this latter being one of the best representatives of the regionalist novel.

[10]In fact, so profound is this ignorance that its contagion has affected such an intelligent reader/researcher as Luis Alberto Sánchez, who, in a brief analysis of Aguilera Malta's *Canal Zone*—and it must be assumed that he actually read the book—refers to, and indeed defines *chombos* as "mulatos locales" (local mulattoes) (*Proceso y contenido de la novela hispanoamericana* [Madrid: Gredos, 1968], p. 465).

[11]Carlos Luis Fallas, *Mamita Yunai*, 5th ed. (San José: Lehmann, 1977), p. 22. All further references to this work appear in the text.

[12]The "something" that he heard and which he translated into his native phonological system as *sontín* is really the Jamaican Creole (Limon Creole) form of the standard English "something," as in: "I have a little something here for lunch...."

[13]*Puerto Limón,* 4th ed. (San José: Editorial Costa Rica, 1976).

[14]Stephen Henderson, *Understanding the New Black Poetry* (New York: Morrow, 1973). All further references to this work appear in the text.

[15]Octavio Paz in *El laberinto de la soledad*, 2nd ed. (México: F.C.E., 1959) has articulated ideas on the significance of the word *"chingar"* to Mexican culture that would make it a "mascon" word according to Henderson's definition. Paz says quite pointedly: "En nuestro lenguaje diario hay un grupo de palabras prohibidas, secretas, sin contenido claro, y a cuya mágica ambiguedad confiamos la expresión de las más brutales o sutiles de nuestras emociones y reacciones" (p. 67).

[16]There are potential dangers in this approach which introduces the delicate matter of the insider/outsider relationship. I am, in a sense, an outsider, not being a native of Central America. However, in another real sense, I am an insider, being a West Indian. It is the "West Indianness" that this analysis seeks to unearth and present as fundamental.

[17]The term "négritude" is formed from a combination of "nègre," the word for black that certainly now has a clearly pejorative connotation, and the suffix "-itude," that signifies the abstract quality or essence.

[18]Cubena (Carlos Guillermo Wilson), *Chombo* (Miami: Universal, 1981), p. 38. All further references to this work appear in the text.

[19]Quince Duncan, *Los cuatro espejos* (San José: Editorial Costa Rica, 1973): *Una canción en la madrugada* (San José: Editorial Costa Rica, 1970); *La paz del pueblo* (San José: Editorial Costa Rica, 1978); and *La rebelión pocomía y otros relatos* (San José: Editorial Costa Rica, 1976). All further references to these works appear in the text.

[20]Cubena (Carlos Guillermo Wilson), "Luna de miel," in *Cuentos del negro Cubena* (Guatemala: Landívar, 1977), pp. 29-44. All further references to this work appear in the text.

[21]Gerardo Maloney, "Testimonios," *Revista Nacional de Cultura,* No. 5 (1976), p. 104.

[22]Abel Pacheco, *Más abajo de la piel* (San José: Editorial Costa Rica, 1972), p. 26. All further references to this work appear in the text.

[23]*El jaspe* (San José: "Repertorio Americano," 1956).

[24]R. F. Cassidy and R. B. Le Page, *Dictionary of Jamaican English,* 2nd ed. (London: Cambridge Univ. Press, 1980). All further references to this work appear in the text.

[25]See Richard L. Jackson, *Black Writers in Latin America* (Albuquerque: Univ. of New Mexico Press, 1979), pp. 176-177.

[26]The intense emotive reactions to typical dietary items probably accounts, more than anything else, for the commercial success of West Indian eating places that have begun to appear in the Washington, D.C. area. Presumably the same phenomenon occurs in other metropolitan centers throughout North America: Toronto, New York, Montreal, Los Angeles, etc.; and throughout the world: London, Paris, Amsterdam, Liverpool, etc.

[27]For more information on these works consult Kenneth Ramchand, *The West Indian Novel and Its Background* (London: Faber and Faber, 1970).

[28]Leonard Barrett, *The Rastafarians* (Boston: Beacon, 1977), p. 17.

[29]Barrett, p. 18.

[30]*Miss Anna's Son Remembers* (Brooklyn, New York: Bayano, 1976), p. 29

[31]Even though the literary language of Afro-Antilleans from Central America is now certainly Spanish with a West Indian flavor, it is legitimate to speculate on the relative fixity or fluidity of this state of affairs. The factors that affect it are many. In the first place there is that ongoing process in the rest of the Caribbean by which creoles and standards jostle for prominence. One school of thought among contemporary linguists holds that the continuua that generally result have had at their two poles the basilectal "deep" creole and the acrolectal "standard" version of the European language. In Central America the scenario has been radically altered by the replacement of Spanish as the acrolectal pole of the "English" Creole continuum.

I have found some data taken from the speech of certain young (fourth generation) West Indian Panamanaian friends which, I think, could support this contention:

a) The teacher didn't "put" the exam = The teacher didn't "give" the exam. (influence of the Spanish, "*poner un examen*" = to "put" an exam = to give an exam).
b) What number you "mark?" = What number did you dial? (influence of the Spanish, "*marcar el número*" = "to mark" the number = to dial the number)

Of course, the forms "*obeahmanes*" and "*galcita*" (from the creole "gal" [girl] + the Spanish " *-cita*" [a diminitive suffix]) can be considered samples of the same basic process.

Indeed, some claim that a process of relexification of creoles has already occured in the Caribbean in the case, for example, of Papiamento, the language of Aruba and Curacao—Dutch owned islands off the coast of Spanish-speaking Venezuela, and culturally as well as demographically in touch with both the English and French-speaking Caribbean. The proponents of the relexification theory sometimes point to the creole language of Dutch-speaking Suriname as an instance of an English Creole that has been "relexified" towards a Dutch acrolect. This language, then, Sranan, would, according to this view, have undergone a process that is exactly analogous to many aspects of the present-day situation of Panamanian English.

CHAPTER THREE

[1]All overt reference to blackness is deliberately suppressed in this novel. Duncan affirms that he did this to demonstrate that he could write a prize-winning novel without "leaning on" the race question. True to his confident predictions, the novel, submitted anonymously, won both the Editorial Costa Rica in-house prize in 1978 and the Aquileo Echeverría national prize for literature the following year. Since this work ignores the West Indian experience, it may not be considered part of the body of West Indian literature in so far as its subject matter is concerned. Of course, on the other hand, it is a very West Indian work since it is written by a West Indian. This question is a fertile one, and I have treated it in a paper, "La estética negra y la novela de Quince Duncan, *Final de calle*," that is yet to be published.

[2]To this list could be added Duncan's thesis for the *Licenciatura* in Latin American Studies, "Novela y sociedad en los años cuarenta," Thesis National Univ. of Costa Rica 1981.

[3]*African Religions and Philosophy*, 2nd ed. (New York: Anchor-Doubleday, 1970), p. 1.

[4]"The African Presence in Caribbean Literature," *Daedalus*, 103, (Spring 1974), 73.

[5]See Quince Duncan and Carlos Meléndez, *El negro en Costa Rica*, 5th ed. (San José: Editorial Costa Rica, 1978), pp. 118-126.

[6]Creole languages in general combine an underlying West African syntax with one or more European lexica.

[7]Shango is the name of an important Yoruba ancestor who has been elevated to the level of "power," "*loa*," or "*orisha*." It is the name given in Trinidad to the traditional West African religion practiced by certain elements of the population.

[8]For a good account of the fashion in which obeah operates in the contemporary Caribbean see Roy S. Bryce Laporte, "Religión folklórica y negros antillanos en la Zona del Canal de Panamá: Estudio de un incidente y su contexto," *Revista Nacional de Cultura*, No. 5 (1976), pp. 61-80. The pattern of behavior revealed in Dr. Bryce Laporte's article is not restricted to Panamanian West Indians, but is exhibited by other Caribbean peoples.

[9]Melville J. Herskovits, *The Myth of the Negro Past* (1941; rpt. Boston: Beacon, 1958), p. 366.

[10]Syncretism is a synchronic as well as a diachronic process that continues to function in contemporary West African Christianity as well. In this regard, John S. Mbiti reports on the important phenomenon of the independent Christian churches, separatist groups which account for "at least one-fifth of the Christians in Africa" today. They represent, in his view "attempts by African peoples to 'indigenize' Christianity and to interpret and apply it in ways that, perhaps spontaneously, render Christianity both practical and meaningful to them" (*African Religious and Philosophy*, p. 304). The phenomenon he describes is surely a case of syncretism. The AfroAmerican sociologist, Bennetta Jules-Rosette concurs with this interpretation, describing the same data as cases of syncretism, in her article on the subject, "Creative Spirituality From Africa to America," *The Western Journal of Black Studies*, 4 (1980), 273-285.

[11]Quince Duncan, *Los cuatro espejos* (San Jose: Editorial Costa Rica, 1973). All further references to this work appear in the text.

[12]Quince Duncan, *La paz del pueblo* (San José: Editorial Costa Rica, 1978). All further references to this work appear in the text.

[13]Juan Rulfo, *Pedro Páramo* (México, Fondo de Cultura Económica, 1955). Any further references to this work appear in the text.

[14]Quince Duncan, "La rebelión pocomía," in *La rebelión pocomía y otros relatos* (San José: Editorial Costa Rica, 1976), pp. 7-12. All further references to this work appear in the text.

[15]Frantz Fanon, *The Wretched of the Earth*, trans. Constance Farrington (Suffolk: Penguin, 1967). See also the following plays by Aimé Césaire:
Et les chiens se taisaient (Paris: Présence Africaine, 1956);
La Tragedie du Roi Christophe, 2nd ed. (Paris: Présence Africaine, 1970);
Une Saison au Congo (Paris: Editions du Seuil, 1973).

[16]This interpretation has to be intuited from a close reading of the novel, the very last line of which refers to the color of Charles's skin: "Una sonrisa profunda iluminó el color de mi piel" (A profound smile illuminated the color of my skin) (p. 163).

[17]Quince Duncan, "La luz del vigía," in *Una canción en la madrugada* (San José: Editorial Costa Rica, 1970), pp. 49-56. All further references to this work appear in the text.

[18]See Leonard Barrett, *The Rastafarians* (Boston: Beacon, 1977), for information on the important role played by religion in slave revolts as well as in post-slavery Black liberation struggles. Barrett expressly shows this role in the Sam Sharpe Rebellion 1831-32, the Morant Bay Rebellion 1865, and the contemporary Rastafarian movement in Jamaica. C. L. R. James, *The Black Jacobins*, 2nd. ed. (New York: Random House, 1963), affirms that voodoo provided the organizational base and the sustaining inspiration for the Haitian Revolution—the first successful revolution in Latin America, and the only successful, fully national, slave revolt in the Americas, and perhaps in all of human history. As regards the contemporary scene, one has only to reflect on the high number of religious leaders who are or have been in the forefront of the Black struggle in the United States: Elijah Muhammed, Martin Luther King, Jesse Jackson, Andrew Young, etc.

[19]See especially Janheinz Jahn, "Ntu: African Philosophy," in *Muntu*, trans. Marjorie Grene (New York: Grove, 1961), pp. 96-120.

[20]The term itself does not come from the West Indian folk tradition. It is a learned form that Duncan encountered in his studies.

[21]*La muerte de Artemio Cruz*, 4th ed. (México: Fondo de Cultura Económica, 1968).

[22]Quince Duncan, "Los mitos ancestrales," in *La rebelión pocomía y otros relatos* (San José: Editorial Costa Rica, 1976), pp. 73-91. All further references to this work appear in the text.

[23]*Palace of the Peacock*, 2nd. ed. (London: Faber and Faber, 1968).

[24]Duncan so indicated to me in an interview, "The Literary World of Quince Duncan: An Interview," that should be published in the near future.

[25]Lamming has expressed these views in lectures of his that I have attended, in particular the one delivered on November 19, 1980 at the Johns Hopkins University in Baltimore, Maryland. The works I have cited are:

H. G. De Lisser, *Jane's Career*, 2nd ed., Caribbean Writers Series, No. 5 (Kingston, 1913; rpt. London: Heinemann, 1972).

C. L. R. James, *Minty Alley* (1936; rpt. London: New Beacon, 1971).
V. S. Naipaul, *A House for Mr. Biswas*, 2nd. ed. New York: Penguin, 1969).
Samuel Selvon, *A Brighter Sun* (1952; rpt. London: Longman, 1971). *The Lonely Londoners* (1956; rpt. Washington, D.C.: Three Continents Press, 1979).
Michael Thelwell, *The Harder They Come* (New York: Grove, 1980).
Richard Wright, *Native Son*, 2nd. ed. (New York: Harper & Row, 1966).
Joseph Zobel, *Black Shack Alley*, trans. Keith Q. Warner (Washington, D.C.: Three Continents Press, 1980).
Any further references to these works appear in the text.

[26]"The Mystic Quest in Caribbean Literature," *The Western Journal of Black Studies*, 5 (1981), 32.

CHAPTER FOUR

[1]Cubena (Carlos Guillermo Wilson), *Cuentos del negro Cubena* (Guatemala: Landívar, 1977). All further references to this work appear in the text.

[2]*Chombo* (Miami: Universal, 1981). All further references to this work appear in the text.

[3]*Pensamientos del negro Cubena* (Los Angeles: n.p., 1977). All further references to this work appear in the text.

[4]It may be pointed out that two highly rated Latin American novels have structures quite similar to *Chombo*, namely, Mariano Azuela, *Los de abajo* (El Paso, 1915-16; rpt. México, D.F.: Fondo de Cultura Económica, 1958); and Alejo Carpentier, *El reino de este mundo*, 2nd ed. (Mexico, D. F.: Compañía General de Ediciones, 1967). Critics generally claim that Azuela's novel makes a significant contribution to Spanish American literary history, initiating the cycle of novels of the Mexican Revolution, and also effectively initiating the new Spanish American novel liberated from slavish dependence on European aesthetic norms. Carpentier's work paved the way for the use of magical realism as the chosen mode for the new Spanish American novel. His novel, like Cubena's and Azuela's, contains very little character development.

[5]The idea expressed here closely reflects that expressed in the following quote from Carpentier's prologue to *El reino de este mundo*: "the story ... has been based on an extremely rigorous historical documentation which not only respects the historical truth of the events, the names of characters—even secondary ones—of places and even of streets, but which conceals beneath its apparent timelessness a minute array of dates and chronologies" (p. 17). The reader is invited to see Henry J. Richards, "Nelson Estupiñán Bass and the Historico-political Novel: From Theory to Praxis," *Afro-Hispanic Review*, 2 (January 1983), 5-12, for an examination of the question of the historical novel in general and as developed by the contemporary black Ecuadorian novelist Nelson Estupiñán Bass.

[6]Richard L. Jackson uses this expression as the title of his chapter on Cubena's work in *Black Writers in Latin America* (Alburqueque: Univ. of New Mexico Press, 1979), pp. 180-190.

[7]I have heard Prof. Brathwaite express this view at several of his public lectures, most notably in Spring 1976 at Claremont College in California.

[8]See Janheinz Jahn, "Ntu: African Philosophy," in *Muntu*, trans. Marjorie Grene (New York: Grove, 1961), pp. 96-120, for a comprehensive and above all accessible treatment of this matter.

[9]Ian I. Smart, "Big Rage and Big Romance," *Caribbean Review*, 10 (Summer 1979), p. 38.

[10]See Ian I. Smart, "The 'tremendismo negrista' in *Cuentos del negro Cubena*," *Studies in AfroHispanic Literature*, 2 (1978), 41-52.

[11]V. S. Naipaul, *Miguel Street*, 2nd ed. (New York: Penguin, 1971); C. L. R. James, *Minty Alley* (1936; rpt. London: New Beacon, 1971); and George Lamming, *In the Castle of My Skin*, 2nd ed. (London: Longman, 1970).

[12]Selwyn R. Cudjoe's essential argument in *Resistance and Caribbean Literature* (Athens, Ohio: Ohio Univ. Press, 1980) is valid for all aspects of Caribbean culture—not just literature—and applies as well to all colonial cultures. Figures such as Marcus Garvey, Stokely Carmichael, Joel

Augustus Rogers, and Claude McKay particularly illustrate the validity of these insights.
  [13]*Confabulario total*, 4th ed. (Mexico, D. F.: Fondo de Cultura Económica, 1966), p. 33.
  [14]"Big Rage," p. 34.

CHAPTER FIVE

[1]Cubena (Carlos Guillermo Wilson), *Pensamientos del negro Cubena* (Los Angeles: n.p., 1977).
  Eulalia Bernard, *Ritmohéroe* (San José: Editorial Costa Rica, 1982). All further references to these two works appear in the text.
  David McField, *En la calle de enmedio* (Managua: Editora Nicaragüense, 1968).

_____ , *Poemas para el año del elefante* (Managua: Artes *Gráficas,* 1970).

[2]*Miss Anna's Son Remembers* (Brooklyn, N.Y.: Bayano, 1976).
  [3]*Más abajo de la piel* (San José: Editorial Costa Rica, 1972).
  [4]*Poesía nicaragüense* (La Habana: Casa de las Américas, 1973).
  [5]"Cuatro poetas o nueve poemas," *Revista Nacional de Cultura*, No. 5 (1976), pp. 98-105. All further references to this little anthology appear in the text.
  [6]"En el marco del Primer Congreso del Negro Panameño," *La República*, 13 de septiembre, 1981, p. 1-E.
  [7]Carlos Guillermo Wilson, "Sinópsis de la poesía afro-panameña," *Afro-Hispanic Review*, 1 (May 1982), 14-16.
  [8]"El idioma inglés y la integración social de los panameños de origen afro-antillano al carácter nacional panameño," *Revista Nacional de Cultura*, No. 5 (1976), p. 41.
  [9]See, for example, Chancellor Williams, *The Destruction of Black Civilization* (Chicago: Third World Press, 1976) or John G. Jackson, *Introduction to African Civilizations* (Secaucus, New Jersey: The Citadel Press, 1970).
  [10]Carlos Russell has written a poem of the same name on this central phenomenon in West Indian existence (*Miss Anna's Son Remembers*, pp. 24-25). Beleño begins *Curundú* with a chapter in a mode similar to Russell's poem, describing the crucial impact of this institution on the consciousness and life of his main character.
  [11]I make the same argument in my article, "A New Panamanian Poet's Promising Quest for Identity: The Case of Gerardo Maloney," *Plantation Society in the Americas*, 1 (1981), 376-386.
  [12]This appears to be the essential thesis of Eric Williams, *Capitalism and Slavery* (1944; rpt. New York: Capricorn, 1966).
  [13]See René Depestre, "Los fundamentos socioculturales de nuestra identidad," *Casa de las Américas*, No. 58 (1970), pp. 26-34.
  [14]See Ivan Van Sertima, *They Came before Columbus* (New York: Random House, 1976), especially pp. 37-70.
  [15]Roberto Márquez and David Arthur McMurray, *Man-Making Words: Selected Poems of Nicolás Guillén* (Amherst: Univ. of Mass. Press, 1972). p. 77.
  [16]Aimé Césaire, *The Tragedy of King Christophe*, trans. Ralph Manheim (New York: Grove, 1969), p. 25.
  [17]Ian I. Smart, "Big Rage and Big Romance: Discovering a New Panamanaian Author," *Caribbean Review*, 10 (Summer 1979), p. 37.
  [18]J. Bekunuru Kubayanda, "The Linguistic Core of Afro-Hispanic Poetry," *Afro-Hispanic Review*, 1 (September 1982), p. 23.

The identification as West Indian in the poetic works that I have studied of Carlos Rigby as well as of David McField is, to my mind, too tenuous to warrant their being considered major figures. Their contribution is more suitably assessed in the schematic terms of the Conclusion.

CHAPTER SIX

[1]G. R. Coulthard, *Race and Colour in Caribbean Literature* (London: Oxford Univ. Press, 1962).

Wilfred G. Cartey, *Black Images* (New York: Teachers College Press, 1970).

Franklin W. Knight, *The Caribbean* (New York: Oxford Univ. Press, 1978).

Selwyn R. Cudjoe, *Resistance and Caribbean Literature* (Athens: Ohio Univ. Press, 1980). All further references to these works appear in the text.

[2]*The Black Jacobins*, 2nd ed. (New York: Random House, 1963), p. 391.

[3]*Capitalism and Slavery* (1944; rpt. New York: Capricorn, 1966).

From Columbus to Castro: The History of the Caribbean 1492-1969 (London: Deutsch, 1970).

[4]"Four Poets of the Greater Antilles," *Caribbean Quarterly*, 2, No. 4 (1952), 8-15.

[5]Donald E. Herdeck et al., *Caribbean Writers* (Washington, D.C.: Three Continents Press, 1979).

Lambros Comitas, ed., *The Complete Caribbeana 1900-1975*, 4 vols. (New York: KTO Press, 1977.

[6]Ian I. Smart, "Discovering the Caribbean: Two Important Research Tools, "*Caribbean Review*, 10 (Summer 1981), 32-34.

[7]*Islands* (London: Oxford Univ. Press, 1969), p. 34.

[8]Isabelo Zenón Cruz, *Narciso descubre su trasero*, 2 vols. (Humacao, P. R.: Furidi, 1974, 1975).

Carlos More, "Cuba the Untold Story," *Présence Africaine*, No. 52 (1964), pp. 177-229.

[9]In support of this claim see, for example, Mervyn C. Alleyne, *Comparative Afro-American* (Ann Arbor: Karoma, 1980).

[10]See Frantz Fanon, *The Wretched of the Earth*, trans. Constance Farrington (Suffolk: Penguin, 1967), especially pp. 27-84.

[11]See Kenneth Ramchand, *The West Indian Novel and Its Background* (London: Faber and Faber, 1970), especially pp. 51-62.

[12]See Ian I. Smart, "The African Heritage in Spanish Caribbean Literature," *The Western Journal of Black Studies*, 5 (1981), 23-31.

[13]Edward Brathwaite's most important work in this respect is *The Arrivants: A New World Trilogy* (London: Oxford Univ. Press, 1973).

[14]*The Harder They Come* (New York: Grove, 1980).

[15]*Brother Man* (London: Jonathan Cape, 1954).

[16]*Black Shack Alley* (Washington, D.C.: Three Continents Press, 1980).

[17]For more on this theory see my article cited in note #12 above.

[18]Lilyan Kesteloot, *"Les Ecrivains noirs de langue française: naissance d'une littérature,"* 4th ed. (Bruxelles: Editions de l'Institute de Sociologie, 1971), especially p. 29.

Bibliography

PRIMARY SOURCES

Aguilera Malta, Demetrio. *Canal Zone.* Santiago, Chile: Ediciones Ercilla, 1935.

Beleño C., Joaquín. *Luna Verda.* [Panamá]: n.p., 1951.

_____. *Gamboa Road Gang.* Panamá: Primer Premio Concurso Ricardo Miró, 1959.

_____. *Curundú.* Panamá. Ministerio de Educación, 1963.

_____. *Flor de banana.* Panamá: Librería Cultural Panameña, 1974.

Bernard, Eulalia. *Ritmohéroe.* San José: Editorial Costa Rica, 1982.

Cubena (Carlos Guillermo Wilson). *Cuentos del negro Cubena.* Guatemala: Landívar, 1977.

_____. *Pensamientos del negro Cubena.* Los Angeles: n.p., 1977.

_____. *Chombo.* Miami: Universal, 1981.

Dobles, Fabián. *El jaspe.* San José: Ediciones "Repertorio Americano," 1956.

_____. *Historias de Tata Mundo.* San José: Editorial Costa Rica, 1966.

_____. *Cuentos de Fabián Dobles.* San José: Editorial Universitaria Centroamericana, 1971.

Duncan, Quince. *Una canción en la madrugada.* San José: Editorial Costa Rica, 1970.

_____. *Los cuatro espejos.* San José: Editorial Costa Rica, 1973.

_____. *La rebelión pocomía y otros relatos.* San José: Editorial Costa Rica, 1976.

_____. *La paz del pueblo.* San José: Editorial Costa Rica, 1978.

_____. *Final de calle.* San José: Editorial Costa Rica, 1981.

Fallas, Carlos Luis. *Mamita Yunai.* 5th ed. San José: Librería Lehmann, 1977.

132

_____ . *Gentes y gentecillas*. 5th ed. San José: Editorial Costa Rica, 1977.

_____ . *Tres cuentos*. 3rd ed. San José: Editorial Costa Rica, 1975.

_____ . *Mi madrina*. 7th ed. San José: Editorial Costa Rica, 1978.

Gutiérrez, Joaquín. *Manglar*. Santiago, Chile: Nascimiento, 1947.

_____ . *Cocorí*. 14th ed. San José: Editorial Costa Rica, 1977.

_____ . *Puerto Limón*. 4th ed. San José: Editorial Costa Rica, 1976.

_____ . *Murámonos Federico*. San José: Editorial Costa Rica, 1973.

León Sánchez, José. *La cattleya negra*. San José: Editorial Costa Rica, 1967.

_____ . *La isla de los hombres solos*. San José: Imprenta Tormo, 1968.

Maloney, Gerardo. "Cuatro poetas o nueve poemas." *Revista Nacional de Cultura*, No. 5 (1976), pp. 98-105.

_____ . "En el marco del Primer Congreso del Negro Panameño." *La República*, 13 de sept. 1981, p. 1-E.

McField, David. *En la calle de enmedio*. Managua: Editora Nicaragüense, 1968.

_____ . *Poemas para el año del elefante*. Managua: Artes Gráficas, 1970.

Pacheco, Abel. *Más abajo de la piel*. San José: Editorial Costa Rica, 1972.

Rigby, Carlos. "Poemas." In *Poesía nicaragüense*. Ed. Ernesto Cardenal. La Habana: Casa de las Américas, 1973, pp. 547-560.

Russell, Carlos E. *Miss Anna's Son Remembers*. Brooklyn, N.Y.: Bayano Publications, 1976.

Sinán, Rogelio. *Cuentos de Rogelio Sinán*. San José: Editorial Universitaria Centroamericana, 1971.

Smith, Walter. "Cuatro poetas o nueve poemas." *Revista Nacional de Cultura*, No. 5 (1976), p. 109.

Smith Fernández, Alberto. "Cuatro poetas o nueve poemas." *Revista Nacional de Cultura*, No. 5 (1976), pp. 106-108.

SELECTED SECONDARY SOURCES

Alleyne, Mervyn C. *Comparative Afro-American: An Historical-Comparative Study of English-Based Afro-American Dialects of the New World*. Ann Arbor: Karoma, 1980.

Arreola, Juan José. *Confabulario.* 4th ed. México, D. F.: Fondo de Cultura Económica, 1966.

Barrett, Leonard. *The Rastafarians: Sound of Cultural Dissonance.* Boston: Beacon, 1977.

Biesanz, John, and Mavis. *The People of Panama.* 1955; rpt. Westport, Conn.: Greenwood Press, 1977.

Brathwaite, Edward. *The Arrivants: A New World Trilogy.* London: Oxford Univ. Press, 1973.

_____ . *Black + Blues.* Havana: Casa de las Américas, 1976.

_____ . "The African Presence in Caribbean Literature." *Daedalus,* 103 (Spring 1974), 73-109.

Bryce Laporte, Roy S. "Religión folklórica y negros antillanos en la Zona del Canal de Panamá: Estudio de un incidente y su contexto." *Revista Nacional de Cultura,* No. 5 (1976), pp. 61-80.

Cantón, Alfredo. *Juventudes exhaustas.* Panamá: n.p., 1963.

Carpentier, Alejo. *El reino de este mundo.* 1949; rpt. México, D.F.: Compañía General de Ediciones, 1967.

Cartey, Wilfred G. *Black Images.* New York: Teachers College Press, 1970.

Cassidy, F. G., and R. B. Le Page. *Dictionary of Jamaican English.* 2nd ed. London: Cambridge Univ. Press, 1980.

Césaire, Aimé. *Cahier d'un retour au pays natal Return to My Native Land.* Trans. Emile Snyder. Paris: Présence Africaine, 1971.

_____ .*Et les chiens se taisaient.* Paris: Présence Africaine, 1956.

_____ . *La Tragédie du Roi Christophe.* 2nd ed. Paris: Présence Africaine, 1970.

_____ . *Une Saison au Congo.* Paris: Editions du Seuil, 1973.

_____ . *Discours sur le colonialisme.* 6th ed. Paris: Présence Africaine, 1973.

Comitas, Lambros, ed. *The Complete Caribbeana 1900-1975.* 4 vols. New York: KTO Press, 1977.

Coulthard, G. R. *Race and Colour in Caribbean Literature.* London: Oxford Univ. Press, 1962.

Cudjoe, Selwyn R. *Resistance and Caribbean Literature.* Athens: Ohio Univ. Press, 1980.

Cyrus, Stanley. *El cuento negrista sudamericano.* Quito: Casa de la Cultura Ecuatoriana, 1973.

134

Davis, Lisa. "Alienación e integración del negro caribeño en la obra reciente de Quince Duncan de Costa Rica." *Casa de las Américas,* No. 124 (1981), pp. 154-158.

Dawkins-Smart, Buena I. "The Conflict-Replacement and Flexibility-Synthesis Models Relative to Language Attitudes and Language Choices of a Panamanian Minority Group." M.A. Paper UCLA 1980.

Depestre, René. "Los fundamentos socioculturales de nuestra identidad." *Casa de las Américas,* No. 58 (1970), pp. 26-34.

Díaz-Sánchez, Ramón. *Cumboto.* Trans. John Upton. Austin: Univ. of Texas Press, 1969.

Duncan, Quince. *El negro en la literatura costarricense.* San José: Editorial Costa Rica, 1975.

_____ , and Carlos Meléndez. *El negro en Costa Rica.* 5th ed. San José: Editorial Costa Rica, 1978.

_____ . "Novela y sociedad en los años cuarenta: Un análisis de la sociedad costarricense desde una perspectiva literaria." Tesis Universidad Nacional 1981.

Ellison, Ralph. *Invisible Man.* 3rd. ed. 1952; rpt. New York: Vintage-Random House, 1972.

Estupiñán Bass, Nelson. *El último río.* Quito: Casa de la Cultura Ecuatoriana, 1966.

Fanon, Frantz. *Black Skins White Masks.* Trans. Charles Lam Markmann. New York: Grove, 1967.

_____ . *The Wretched of the Earth.* Trans. Constance Farrington. Suffolk: Penguin, 1967.

Flores, Justin. *The Garifuna Story Now and Then.* California: n.p., 1979.

Frazier Clemons, Brenda. "A Review of *Chombo* by Cubena." *Afro-Hispanic Review,* 1 (1981), 33.

Fuentes, Carlos. *La muerte de Artemio Cruz.* 4th ed. Mexico, D.F.: Fondo de Cultura Económica, 1968.

Gallegos, Rómulo. *Pobre negro.* 6th ed. Buenos Aires: Espasa-Calpe Argentina, 1965.

Harris, Wilson. *Palace of the Peacock.* 2nd ed. London: Faber and Faber, 1968.

_____ . *Tradition, the Writer and Society; Critical Essays.* London: New Beacon, 1967.

Henderson, Stephen. *Understanding the New Black Poetry.* New York: Morrow, 1973.

Herdeck, Donald, et al. *Caribbean Writers: A Bio-Bibliographical-Critical Encyclopedia.* Washington, D.C.: Three Continents Press, 1979.

Herskovits, Melville J. *The Myth of the Negro Past.* 1941; rpt. Boston: Beacon, 1958.

Horowitz, Michael M., ed. *Peoples and Cultures of the Caribbean.* New York: The Natural History Press, 1971.

Jackson, John G. *Introduction to African Civilizations.* Secaucus, New Jersey: The Citadel Press, 1970.

Jackson, Richard L. *The Black Image in Latin American Literature.* Albuquerque: Univ. of New Mexico Press, 1976.

_____ . *Black Writers in Latin America.* Albuquerque: Univ. of New Mexico Press, 1979.

Jahn, Janheinz. *Muntu: The New African Culture.* Trans. Marjorie Grene. New York: Grove, 1961.

James, C. L. R. *Minty Alley.* 1936; rpt. London: New Beacon, 1971.

_____ . *The Black Jacobins: Toussaint L'Ouverture and the San Domingo Revolution.* 2nd ed. New York: Vintage-Random House, 1963.

Jules-Rosette, Bennetta. "Creative Spirituality from Africa to America: Cross-Cultural Influences in Contemporary Religious Forms." *The Western Journal of Black Studies,* 4 (1980), 273-285.

Kagame, Alexis. *La Philosophie bantu-rwandaise de l'être.* Bruxelles: Académie Royale des Sciences Coloniales, 1956.

Kesteloot, Lilyan. *Les Ecrivains noirs de langue française: naissance d'une littérature.* 4th ed. Bruxelles: Editions de l'Institut de Sociologie, 1971.

Khan, Ismith. *The Obeah Man.* London: Hutchinson, 1964.

Knight, Franklin W. *The Caribbean: The Genesis of a Fragmented Nationalism.* New York: Oxford Univ. Press, 1978.

Kubayanda, J. B. "The Linguistic Core of Afro-Hispanic Poetry." *Afro-Hispanic Review,* 1 (Sept. 1982), 21-26.

Lamming, George. *In The Castle of My Skin.* 1953; rpt. London: Longman, 1970.

Lewis, Lancelot. *The West Indian in Panama: Black Labor in Panama, 1850-1914.* Washington, D.C.: Univ. Press of the Americas, 1980.

Lowe-Ocran, Melva. "El idioma inglés y la integración social de los panameños de origen afro-antillano al carácter nacional panameño." *Revista Nacional de Cultura*, No. 5 (1976), pp. 22-43.

Manheim, Ralph, trans. *The Tragedy of King Christophe*. By Aimé Césaire. New York: Grove, 1969.

Márquez, Roberto, and David Arthur McMurray. *Man-Making Words: Selected Poems of Nicolás Guillén*. Amherst: Univ. of Massachusetts Press, 1972.

Mbiti, John S. *African Religions and Philosophy*. 2nd. ed. New York: Anchor-Doubleday, 1970.

Métraux, Alfred. *Voodoo in Haiti*. Trans. Hugo Charteris. 1959; rpt. New York: Schocken, 1972.

Miró Rodrigo. *La literatura panameña*. Panamá: Serviprensa, 1976.

More, Carlos. "Cuba: The Untold Story." *Présence Africaine*, No. 52 (1964), pp. 177-229.

Morton, Allen G. "The Private Schools of the British West Indians in Panama." Diss. George Peabody College for Teachers 1966.

Naipaul, V. S. *Miguel Street*. London: André Deutsch, 1959.

_____ . *A House for Mr. Biswas*. 2nd ed. New York: Penguin, 1969.

Nettleford, Rex. *Identity Race and Protest in Jamaica*. New York: Morrow, 1972.

Ortiz, Adalberto. *Juyungo*. Guayaquil: Librería Cervantes, 1942.

Patterson, Orlando H. *The Children of Sisyphus*. Kingston: Bolivar Press, 1971.

Paz, Octavio. *El laberinto de la soledad*. 2nd ed. Mexico, D.F.: Fondo de Cultura Económica, 1959.

Pernett y Morales, Rafael. *Loma ardiente y vestida de sol*. Panamá: Ediciones INAC, 1977.

Ramchand, Kenneth. *The West Indian Novel and Its Background*. London: Faber and Faber, 1970.

Ramírez, Manuel, III., "Recognizing and Understanding Diversity: Multiculturalism and the Chicano Movement in Psychology." In *Chicano Psychology*. Ed. Joe L. Martínez, Jr. New York: Academic Press, 1977, pp. 343-353.

Revilla, Angel. *Panameñismos*. Panamá: Impresora Roysa, 1976.

Richards, Henry J. "Nelson Estupiñán Bass and the Historico-Political Novel: From Theory to Praxis." *Afro-Hispanic Review*, 2 (January 1983), 5-12.

137

Rigsby, Gregory U. "The Mythic Quest in Caribbean Literature." *The Western Journal of Black Studies*, 5 (1981), 32-40.

Rout, Leslie B., Jr. *The African Experience in Spanish America: 1502 to the Present Day.* Cambridge: Cambridge Univ. Press, 1976.

Roumain, Jacques. *Gouverneurs de la rosée.* Port-au-Prince, 1944; rpt. Paris: Les Editeurs Français Rénuis, 1964.

Rulfo, Juan. *Pedro Páramo.* México, D.F.: Fondo de Cultura Económica, 1955.

Sartre, Jean-Paul. "Orphée Noir." In *Anthologie de la nouvelle poésie nègre et malgache.* Ed. L. Sédar Senghor. 3rd ed. Paris: Presses Universitaires de France, 1972, pp. ix-xliv.

Saz del, Agustín D. *Antología general de la poesía panameña (siglos xix-xx).* Barcelona: Bruguera, 1974.

Selvon, Samuel. *A Brighter Sun.* 1952; rpt. London: Longman, 1971.

_____ . *The Lonely Londoners.* 1956; rpt. Washington, D.C.: Three Continents Press, 1979.

Sepúlveda, Mélida Ruth. *El* [Panama]: *Canal en la novelística panameña.* Caracas: Universidad Católica "Andrés Bello" Centro de Investigaciones Literarias, 1975.

Shapiro, Norman R., ed. and trans. *Negritude: Black Poetry from Africa and the Caribbean.* New York: October House, 1970.

Smart, Ian I. "The 'tremendismo negrista' in *Cuentos del negro Cubena.*" *Studies in Afro-Hispanic Literature*, 2 (1978). 41-52.

_____ . "Big Rage and Big Romance: Discovering a New Panamanian Author." *Caribbean Review*, 8 (Summer 1979), 34-38.

_____ . "Nicolás Guillén's *Son* Poem: An African Contribution to Contemporary Caribbean Poetics." *CLA Journal*, 23 (1980), 352-363.

_____ . "The African Heritage in Spanish Caribbean Literature." *The Western Journal of Black Studies*, 5 (1981), 23-31.

_____ . "Discovering the Caribbean: Two Important Research Tools." *Caribbean Review*, 10 (Summer 1981), 32-34.

_____ . "A New Panamanian Poet's Promising Quest for Identity: The Case of Gerardo Maloney." *Plantation Society in the Americas*, 1 (1981), 376-386.

_____ . "Religious Elements in the Narrative of Quince Duncan." *Afro-Hispanic Review*, 1 (May 1982), 27-31.

Taylor, Douglas Mac Rae. *The Black Carib of British Honduras.* New York: Wenner-Green Foundation for Anthropological Research, Inc., 1951.

Thelwell, Michael. *The Harder They Come*. New York: Grove, 1980.

Valdés-Cruz, Rosa E. *La poesía negroide en América*. New York: Las Américas, 1970.

Van Sertima, Ivan. *They Came before Columbus: The African Presence in Ancient America*. New York: Random House, 1976.

Weil, Thomas E., et al. *Area Handbook for Panama*. Washington, D.C.: U.S. Govt. Printing Office, 1972.

Welch, Winston R. "Evolución de la población negroide en Panamá." An unpublished paper.

Westerman, George W. *Los inmigrantes antillanos en Panamá*. Panama: INAC, 1980.

Williams, Chancellor. *The Destruction of Black Civilization*. Chicago: Third World Press, 1976.

Williams, Eric. *Capitalism and Slavery*. 1944; rpt. New York: Capricorn, 1966.

_____ . *From Columbus to Castro: The History of the Caribbean 1492-1969*. London: André Deutsch, 1970.

_____ . "Four Poets of the Greater Antilles." *Caribbean Quarterly*, 2, No. 4 (1952), 8-15.

Wilson, Carlos Guillermo (Cubena). "Aspectos de la prosa panameña." Diss. UCLA 1975.

_____ . "Sinópsis de la poesía afro-panameña." *Afro-Hispanic Review*, 1 (May 1982), 14-16.

Wright, Richard. *Native Son*. 2nd ed. New York: Harper and Row, 1966.

Zapata Olivella, Manuel. *Chambacú, corral de negros*. 9th ed. Medellín, Colombia: Bedout, 1981.

Zenón Cruz, Isabelo. *Narciso descrube su trasero: El negro en la cultura puertorriqueña*. 2 vols. Humacao, Puerto Rico: Editorial Furidi, 1974, 1975.

Zobel, Joseph. *Black Shack Alley*. Trans. Keith Q. Warner. Washington, D.C.: Three Continents Press, 1980.

INDEX

140

A

Accompong: 73
Africa: 1, 44, 66, 88, 106, 107, 113,
114; "Africa seen realistically":
103-105
African: 26, 32, 33, 43, 44, 51, 54, 55,
63, 64, 67, 70, 72, 73, 74, 75,
76, 82, 83, 84, 89, 93, 94, 95,
99, 103, 105, 106, 108, 112,
113, 114, 124; heritage: 12, 49,
53, 103, 111, 112; philosophy
and religion: 33, 51, 52, 61, 62,
82, 94; presence: 10, 11, 12, 83,
112
Africanisms: 48
Africanity: 12, 120
Africanness: 83, 112
Afro–: 32, 48, 60, 65, 93, 115, 121
Afro-American: 42, 48, 56, 60, 66,
124
afro-antillano panameño: 10, 119
Afro-Antillean: 34, 38, 39, 64, 65, 69,
98, 106, 107, 123
Afro-Caribbean: 24, 27, 28, 30, 32,
33, 34, 40, 43, 45, 46, 47, 52,
64, 119
afro-caribeño: 119
"*afrolatindígena*": 27
Agayú: 82
Aguilera Malta, Demetrio: 30, 39;
Canal Zone: 20-21, 29, 33, 120
Alabama (Mobile): 77
Alaska: 93
albino: 75, 76
Ali, Muhammad: 106
Alleyne, Mervyn C.: 121, 127
America, Americas: 31, 32, 73, 74, 75,
81, 83, 89, 93, 95, 96, 101, 103,
105, 124

American: 39, 56, 79, 95, 101, 107
Amerindian: 112
Amsterdam: 84, 93, 122
ancestors: 44, 61, 62, 72, 74, 75, 79,
83, 91, 94, 103, 114, 123
Anglophone: 10, 11, 12, 50, 97, 109,
114
Anglophone Caribbean: 13, 28, 44,
70, 79, 87, 106, 109, 115, 116,
119, 121
Anglophone West Indian: 43
Anglo-Saxon: 120
Angola: 104, 105, 112
antillais: 12
antillanismo: 50
antillano: 10, 12, 14, 27, 91, 92, 119,
120
"antillano de verdad": 36
Arreola, Juan José: 86, 126
Aruba: 123
Ashanti: 48, 53, 61, 62, 75, 93, 106
Atlantic: 22, 94
Azania: 104
Aztec: 75
Azuela, Mariano: 125

B

Balzac, Honoré de: 69
Bantu: 74, 103
Barrett, Leonard: 48, 53, 122, 124
Beleño, Joaquín C.: 13-19, 20, 23, 25,
27, 28, 30, 32, 36, 38, 39, 40,
41, 43, 49, 98; *Curundú:* 14-16,
25, 28, 32, 36, 38, 45, 120, 121,
126; *Flor de banana:* 120; *Gamboa Road Gang:* 13, 14, 17-19,
28, 31, 32, 120; *Luna verde:* 14,
16-17, 28, 31, 38, 120, 121
Belize, Belizian: 5, 9, 10, 112

Bibliographic Note on Author

A native of Trinidad and Tobago, Ian I. Smart is currently an associate professor of Spanish at Howard University in Washington, D.C. He earned a doctorate in Spanish from UCLA (1975), having taken his B.A. and M.A. degrees at University College Dublin (Ireland) and the National Autonomous University of Mexico (Mexico City) respectively. He writes extensively on pan-Caribbean literature and culture. His wife, Buena Isidra, is a native of Panama. Dr. Smart is a co-founder of the *Afro-Hispanic Review* and serves as Managing Editor.